Wilkinson Waldorf Curriculum Series

# The Norse Stories and their Significance



Roy Wilkinson

RSCP

The publisher is grateful for the encouragement and support of Robert Dulaney in making this new edition possible.

The name Waldorf really belongs only to the first school of its type, the one founded by Rudolf Steiner in Stuttgart, Germany for the children of the workers at the Waldorf-Astoria factory. It has since been adopted as the generic name of schools conducted according to Rudolf Steiner's recommendations. In place of Waldorf some establishments call themselves Rudolf Steiner schools. Others take a distinctive name and add Waldorf or Rudolf Steiner in some connection as a subtitle.



Revised 1999

ISBN 0-945803-43-5



Book orders may be made through Rudolf Steiner College Bookstore. Tel. 916-961-8729, FAX 916-961-3032.

Rudolf Steiner College Press
9200 Fair Oaks Boulevard
Fair Oaks, CA 95628, U.S.A.

# Contents

# Foreword

At first sight the Norse stories appear to be a weird and wonderful collection of tales, illogical in sequence and with no coherent theme. The reason for this may lie partly in the oral tradition and partly in the fact that they come from various sources. In the course of time, too, it is possible that the texts did not suit some editors or publishers and therefore 'improvements' have been made which alter the sense.

However that may be, there is in the Norse stories a great depth of knowledge and, fragmentary as they are, they are probably relics of old Mystery wisdom. They present a picture of evolution, of the creation and development of the human being and his connection with higher beings; they show the human being's struggle with adverse powers, the fading of the old world conception and the birth of the ego which leads to new powers of perception; they show the loss of spiritual vision and the consequent catastrophe (Götterdämmerung); but out of catastrophe comes new hope and new life emerges. The stories hint at the coming of Christ but they also show that humanity must suffer before the Christ impulse takes hold.

Götterdämmerung, the Twilight of the Gods, the Day of Ragnarok—these are different expressions for the great catastrophe which people felt would come. It is the disappearance of spiritual vision, yet the old visionary powers had to disappear in order that the human being might develop individuality and freedom. These are the themes of the stories but they are not portrayed in concepts; they are given in imaginative pictures. It is difficult for the modern mind to grasp this.

In the course of evolution the state of the human mind has changed, just as it changes in the course of a single human life. Today we may speak of retarding forces. To the Norse peoples that would be an incomprehensible abstraction. They experienced retarding forces as giants; a storm at sea as the activity of the sea-serpent; their own ego-consciousness as the figure of Thor. Loki is the Nordic Lucifer. Balder's death is the loss of spiritual vision.

The people among whom these stories originated had a particular outlook on life. It was not the acceptance of fate as is found in the East but of life as a challenge. They were imbued with a sense of adventure and courage to face and overcome life's vicissitudes through the power of their own developing ego. They were the forerunners of the Teutonic age, the age of Europe.

What is sometimes described as an external event can also be an experience of the soul. When we use the expression 'being under a cloud' in the sense of being depressed or threatened, we use it as a figure of speech. To the Norseman the cloud would be real.

Fairy Tales present similar, imaginative pictures. They portray soul experiences and spiritual truths. So do some of the Biblical stories but a special sort of knowledge is essential to understand them. The key to understanding is to be found in the spiritual scientific work of Rudolf Steiner, to which he gave the name Anthroposophy (Knowledge of Man). The explanations given here are founded for the most part on Rudolf Steiner's indications but it is obvious that what is here presented in condensed form will be much more fully understood by further reference to his work.

*Norse Stories and their Significance* complements the author's work on Fairy Tales and Old Testament Stories. They all have a particular bearing on education. All such stories are spiritual food for children. The Fairy Tales are suitable for children at an early age, about five onwards. At the age of nine children develop a greater interest in earthly matters as well as in themselves as individuals. The Old Testament Stories present an objective picture of this development. The Norse Stories are a logical sequence. They portray a further coming to earth and ego development. Such imaginative pictures strengthen the inner being of the child and are eminently suitable for children about ten years old. This sequence of stories has been used in all the schools which base themselves on Rudolf Steiner's educational indications. The present work will be of particular value to teachers preparing to teach these stories or looking to find stories from other cultures bringing comparable spiritual content.

The teacher is recommended to sample various editions of the Norse stories in order to find those which appeal best to him or her. Some are listed in the Bibliography but there may be others unknown to the author. This book contains only short versions of the stories and explanations and it should be pointed out that the explanations are only for adults. Children should live in the imaginative content of the story but the teacher or whoever is concerned should understand the background of what he or she is relating.

As in the case of the other books mentioned, the writer does not claim infallibility or that his explanations are the only ones. There may be other, equally valid, interpretations. He is also aware that some details remain unexplained. There is, however, very little literature available on this subject, and it is to be hoped that these notes, produced over a number of years of study, will be useful.

R. Wilkinson

Forest Row, E. Sussex, England

# The Creation

Before the beginning of time there was no earth, no sky, no sea, no grass, no trees, only a yawning void known as Ginnungengap. To the north was the home of mist, Niflheim, packed with ice and snow, out of which flowed twelve rivers from the spring, Hvergelmir. The water flowed into the void and turned to ice. To the south was a region of burning heat, the home of fire, Muspelheim. The warm air from Muspelheim floated over the ice and melted it and out of it came the form of the giant, Ymir. He sweated and out of his body oozed other giants.

At the farthest end of Muspelheim was Surtur, waiting, with flaming sword, to destroy men and gods at the day of doom.

As, near Muspelheim, more ice melted, the form of a cow appeared, Audumla, and from her udder flowed four streams of milk.

Ymir fed from her milk and Audumla licked the salty ice-blocks for her nourishment. One evening, as she licked, a head appeared through the melting ice, then a whole body. This was Buri, one of the gods, whose grandchildren were Odin, Vili and Ve. (The Norsemen called this new race of gods the Aesir and they looked upon Ymir as evil.) Rivalry developed between the gods and giants which led to the death of Ymir and his like although one, Bergelmir, escaped with his wife. From them are descended the Storm giants and the Jotuns, or Rock giants.

Odin and his brothers threw the body of Ymir into the middle of Ginnungengap and shaped earth, sea and sky from it. They made a great mill and ground the flesh of Ymir to make soil. They made mountains from his bones, rocks from his teeth and jaws, trees from his hair, lakes and seas from his blood. His great skull became the arching sky and his brains the clouds. The sky was supported by four dwarfs placed on the four corners of the ends of the earth.

In the course of time, gods, giants and other beings have left their mark. There was a black giant who had a daughter called Night. She married three times. She had a son, a daughter who was called Day, and another called Earth. Earth became the mother of one of the most famous of the Aesir, Thor. Odin put Night in a dark chariot drawn by a black horse called Frosty-Mane, Day he put in a chariot drawn by a white steed known as Shining-Mane.

The gods put a ring of sea around the earth. They made stars from the floating sparks of Muspelheim and put sun and moon in their appointed places.

A stranger whose name was Mundilfari had two beautiful children to whom he gave the names of Sun and Moon. The gods were annoyed at this presumption and Odin put them in the sky to drive the chariots. The wicked giants were angry at this and sent two hungry wolves, the sons of a giantess, to pursue them. The time will come when they catch them and every time there is an eclipse we can see how near they come.

There was now a golden age and the gods passed their time with happy games, throwing the dice and such things, but a shadow fell on their happiness. Three strange womanly figures from ancient times appeared. They were the Norns whose father was Mimir, the Ancient One, who lived before ever this story began. They know the fate of men and now announced that a new age must come.

The gods met to consult with one another. They became aware of creepy things in the flesh of Ymir and the gods transformed them into dwarfs, gave them understanding and form so that they were similar to human beings. Some were sent to live in the earth, some in caves and some behind mountain walls. Mimir was appointed to be their leader.

Three of the gods, Odin, Honir and Lodur, were once walking by the seashore when they came across two trees which, like all such, had been formed from Ymir's hair. These two trees were an Ash and an Elm. The two trees had no power or destiny and the gods created the first man and the first woman from them. Odin, the greatest of the three, gave them breath and soul; Honir gave them a mind and thus the power of forming ideas; Lodur, blood, stature and pigmentation. They were named Ask and Embla. But who now are Honir and Lodur, and what of Odin's other companions, Vili and Ve? All we know at the moment is that different gods have different tasks and sometimes gods, like human beings, change their natures.

The earth lay within the ring of sea and in the middle the gods prepared a place called Midgard in which the human beings could dwell. From Ymir's eyebrows they built a great wall as a boundary beyond which the giants had to live. Their home was known as Jotunheim. Elves, fairies and other such beings of earlier creation also lived beyond the bounds of Midgard. Their home was a region called Elfland but they could easily visit Midgard where they taught the birds to sing, watered the flowers and danced with the butterflies. Not far away there was also a region known as Svartalfheim which means 'Land of the Dark Elves' and here another race of dwarfs dwelt.

In Jotunheim was the well of Mimir, the Well of Wisdom, which has a story for itself.

Above Midgard the gods built their own dwelling, Asgard, with a rainbow bridge joining it to Midgard.

Deep below all other worlds, so the Norsemen believed, was the Realm of Hela where the souls of the dead were judged before they were allowed to continue their journey. The virtuous ones were happy and drank from the horn of Urd which gave them joy and strength; but those who had done evil, the murderers, the profaners of temples, had to pass through regions where they suffered tortures according to their misdeeds.

*In his* Outline of Occult Science *Rudolf Steiner describes three stages of planetary evolution before the present system came into being. Between each stage there is a dissolution of what had been, followed by a new construction. The transition period could be considered chaos in its original sense.*

*The yawning void of the Norse stories, Ginnungengap, represents this chaos, the great deep of primordial substance after three stages of planetary development, out of which the earth is born. It is the same as the Biblical 'without form and void', a spaceless, timeless condition, a chaos of formative forces over which (in the Bible) the Spirit of God moved. It has no physical form or structure. The kingdoms of nature are not differentiated. The human being exists only in spirit.*

*Two formative cosmic processes are at work; one, consolidating; the other, dissolving. These are the result of divine activity.*

*In the Bible the two forces are referred to as heaven and earth but what is really indicated are two focal points, two centres of influence. In the Norse mythology one of these forces is represented as flowing from Niflheim in the north, creating layers of ice. The other comes from Muspelheim in the south and melts it, As a result of the working together of these forces, two beings emerge: in the northern part of what had been the void, Ymir, the giant; in the south, Audumla, the cow. These events represent development from a cosmic potential to the beginning of physical conditions. Ymir is the undifferentiated substance; Audumla, the sustaining, active, life force.*

*Surtur is a high ranking spiritual being who has remained behind in his development. One could think of him as the archetype of evil.*

*No information is given concerning the origin of Buri and the assumption must be that he was one of the divine beings in existence before the events of Ginnungengap. We know from other stories that Ymir had three ancestors and we can assume that these refer to the three earlier conditions of earth. In these there were creative gods who withdrew but handed their work to others. Odin, Vili and Ve are therefore gods of a lower rank who continue the work already started.*

*The gods kill Ymir (and his offspring) and form the world from his body, i.e. they transform the spiritual substance and begin to form from it the physical world. One giant escapes in a boat with his wife and from him descend the Storm giants and the Jotuns (the Rock giants) i.e. two giant races.*

*Giants, in the context of these stories, represent old forces which are negative in their influence. The Storm giants are those related to passions and urges in the soul; the Jotuns, or Rock giants, to the forces of growth—in their case, to non-growth, i.e. hardening, consolidating.*

*In the process of creation, sun, moon and stars were at first spiritual entities. They densified. The Old Testament story says that sun, moon and stars were created on the fourth day, yet light, day and night, the firmament, dry land and the seas, were created earlier. At the end of the creation period the Lord God organised the seasons. Fixing the position of the heavenly bodies signifies the ordering of the cosmos. Day, night and earth are manifestations out of the original chaos. The Norse mythology does not put it quite so clearly but the story is essentially the same. It also points out how the human being has to work with the heav-*

*enly influences, would actually like to conquer them. Hence the picture of human children driving the chariots of the sun and the moon.*

*The peoples of the north had a premoniton of godless times to come which is referred to as the day of Ragnarok, the day of doom (Götterdämmerung). The pursuit of the sun by the wolves is a sign of evil times ahead. These peoples still had clairvoyant vision. Day, night, sun and moon were not the clear objects of our modern minds; neither were other objects of nature but the Norse peoples experienced them as objects peopled or motivated by spiritual beings.*

*There is, however, another aspect to this story of creation.*

*The macrocosmic process described as the spring and the twelve rivers of Niflheim is duplicated in the microcosmic human brain and the twelve cranial nerves. The meaning of Hvergelmir is something like 'a whirling in the helm', i.e. the brain within the skull. Ymir is the prototype of the nerve-sense human being with his centre in the head. With the head is connected the new process of cognition and a new consciousness. But thinking is a cold process, hence Ymir is looked upon as evil.*

*The Muspelheim influence is the cosmic creative, life-giving force and Audumla represents the metabolic processes in the human being.*

*Thus as a mirror and as a creation of the two forces of Niflheim and Muspelheim, we see Ymir and Audumla. Together they represent the human being in a twofold aspect, as they were also experienced in other cultures, i.e. the sphinx in Egypt and the centaur in Greece: human above, animal below.*

*Further activity by Audumla results in the appearance of Buri and, in due course, his grandchildren, Odin, Vili and Ve. The role of this trinity in the further development of the human being will be explained later, but here we note the number: three. The view of a twofold human being is correct as far as it goes, but humans have another attribute. The extremes of nerve and metabolism, head and limbs, have an intermediary system of rhythmic and heart forces. Their development is connected with physical evolution.*

*Once upon a time there was a great continent where the Atlantic ocean now rolls. It was called Atlantis and people of the period were differently constituted from those of a later date. In Atlantis the process of obtaining nourishment was relatively simple—a sort of breathing in—*

*but with the change to eating food a different metabolism developed and, in turn, a means of distributing the products through the organism, hence the development of heart and blood system.*

*The gods now take a break. One is reminded of the Sabbath in the Bible story but the Norse divinities are now stimulated to further activity by the visit of the Norns. These beings are the ones who understand fate. It is the fate of human beings to become free and independent but for this they need a central point of power within themselves, a force which gives them their own direction, namely an ego. This is what the Norns announce.*

*Immediately following this visit of the Norns the gods become aware of creepy-crawlies in the flesh of Ymir and change them into dwarfs.*

*The creation of the dwarfs is somewhat enigmatical. Dwarfs are representative of nature beings whose cleverness is intuitive. The picture suggests that forces of metamorphosis are at work in the earth-body out of which intelligent beings evolve and exist in their own right; but the picture could also be symbolic with regard to human development. Metamorphosis is an essential prelude to receiving new powers. The picture could, therefore, represent a preliminary to the next event which is the bestowal of those qualities which are the essentials of the human being.*

*The story now concentrates, as in the Bible, on the creation of one pair, samples, so to speak. The necessary preliminary work for making humans into beings of the earth has now been completed and the gods can pour their gifts, which will make them so, into the prepared moulds.*

*The gods find two trees. The names Ash and Elm (Askr and Embla) remind us of Adam and Eve.*

*As the human physical body evolved out of the Ymir substance, so also the etheric body, the life forces. Trees were formed from Ymir's hair so the two trees represent the prototype physical and etheric into which the gods can incorporate the spirit.*

*The story here again parallels that of the Bible. In Genesis are two stories of creation. The first is a spiritual creation; the second is a consolidation of forms and actual endowment with the spirit. All this is still however, non-physical. One might say it is prototype physical. The human being only becomes an earth being through the Fall, the Luciferic temptation.*

*In the Norse stories there is no account of the Fall. The gods themselves give the human being the necessary equipment for earthly existence.*

*There is a certain difficulty here since there are two versions of the story. The personalities and their gifts are as follows:*

| | | |
|---|---|---|
| 1 | *Odin* | *Breath and Soul* |
| | *Honir* | *Mind and the power of forming Ideas* |
| | *Lodur* | *Blood, Stature and Pigmentation* |
| 2 | *Odin* | *Spirit and Life* |
| | *Vili* | *Movement, Intelligence* |
| | *Ve* | *Stature, Hearing, Sight, Speech* |

*We note immediately that there is a threefoldness which is approximately equated to the three soul forces of thinking, feeling and willing. Perhaps there was a difference in the feeling in the peoples concerned or they experienced the deities in different ways. (Later Hoder seems to take the place of Honir and Loki of Lodur. It means that the senses become materially orientated and self becomes predominant in the fire of the blood.) In any case, these gifts denote the advent of the ego.*

*Midgard is now formed for human beings, i.e. they come to earth. Significantly, Midgard is bounded by a wall made from Ymir's eyebrows. This region has a particular significance in that the eyes of human beings are the mirror of their souls. It is where their humanity is expressed. The top of the head resembles the dome of heaven, Ymir's skull; the jaw is connected with Audumla, the metabolic system. In between is a 'middle'.*

*The gods have their own dwelling place, Asgard.*

*The nether region obviously refers to purgatory. It is an established belief that the souls of the dead must be cleansed before they can make progress in the spiritual world. The torments suffered are really those which have been self-inflicted.*

## Yggdrasil, the World Tree

Following the creation of worlds and men and women, a seeress had a vision. She saw a great Ash tree surrounded by a white mist. It stretched over all that was, and all the regions of the new world were within it. Its topmost branches reached into the heavens. It was called Yggdrasil.

It had three roots. One reached to the spring, Hvergelmir, in Niflheim. Under this root lived the dragon, Nidhogg, who gnawed at the root. Serpents also inhabited this region. The spring was fed by the drops of dew which fell from the antlers of Odin's stag in Valhalla. The stag ate the twigs of the great tree to obtain his nourishment.

The second root stretched to Mimir's well in Jotunheim. Mimir could remember everything that had happened in the world. Drinking daily from this well gave him his wisdom.

A third root reached to Asgard and the well of Urd, tended by the three fates. These were known as the Norns and their names were Urd, Verdandi and Skuld. Urd could see the past; Verdandi, the present and Skuld, the future. Nearby, the Aesir met in their council chamber, the Hall of justice. The work of the Norns was to spin the fate of human beings. They also sprinkled the great tree daily with water from their well and some trickled down to the earth below, feeding every living thing. Some turned to honey and the bees fed on it. On the water floated a pair of swans.

At the top of the tree there was an eagle, keeping watch on everything and reporting to Odin. Between the eagle's eyes sat a falcon.

A squirrel, Ratatosk, ran up and down the tree carrying insults and making mischief between the eagle and Nidhogg.

No-one can tell what the tree suffered. Four stags pastured in the branches, eating off the buds and damaging the tree.

Deeply hidden in the tree were the seeds of the future. When the question was asked as to who would survive the end of the world, the answer was, 'Lif and Lifthrasir, who would be in Mimir's grove'. But who are Lif and Lifthrasir? And what was

Mimir's grove? These were secrets at the time but it was said that Lif and Lifthrasir were the names of an unborn man and woman who would found a new race.

*According to Rudolf Steiner the Nordic peoples experienced the forces of the spiritual world working in their organisms and these are what appear in the picture of the tree. Yggdrasil is an imagination of the tree of life, or of the human being, who has to find within him- or herself the strength on which the world order rests. It is a picture of 'I am'.*

*The Ash tree is bi-sexual and the fact that an Ash tree is specified means that it represents the male/female human being, not just the male. The white mist is the mist of Atlantis and the tree appears out of this background as representing the new ego-endowed human being. Uprightness is symbolic of the ego. The name itself, Yggdrasil, means ego-bearer. The topmost branches are in the heavens, i.e. the human being's highest faculties are spiritual.*

*The tree has three roots, each fed by a spring. Human nature is threefold.*

*The head and the twelve nerves were already mentioned. The root in Niflheim by the well of Hvergelmir signifies the awakening of the head forces to consciousness, Niflheim is the old world of Atlantis from which the head thinkers emigrated. The origin of these forces lies however in the spiritual world, hence the picture of the streams being fed by the drops from the stag's antlers. Gnawing at the root is Nidhogg and serpents are present. One is reminded of the serpent in the paradise story, one result of whose influence was conscious sexual activity. The dragon signifies the dangers of excess, the unloosening of bodily passions which affect the thinking. Consciousness in sexual relationships leads also to tribal consciousness, an enclosed society having a group ego. The awakening of head forces is a step towards individual ego-consciousness.*

*The second root leads to Mimir's well in Jotunheim. (Mimir =memory.) The well contains primeval wisdom, knowledge of the origin of all things, i.e. the creative word. All things were created by the divine word which is reflected in the human being in his power of speech. Speech is something which lifts the human being above the animal world, i.e. it is connected with ego-consciousness. Odin has to reshape it for the new-developing human being and that story will follow in due course.*

*Jotunheim is the home of the giants, i.e. forces of old Atlantis. In changing to a new age the power of speech developed. Speech is connected with breathing and breathing with the rhythmic system. So here is an indication of the heart and chest system.*

*The third root is in Asgard, by Urd's well. This is where destiny is formed. Only an ego being can have a destiny and his destiny is connected with the gods, hence the presence here of the gods' Hall of Justice. Destiny is formed by deeds, deeds by the limbs. The present depends on the past, the future on the present. Here the law of karma is demonstrated, i.e. the results of deeds or attitudes in one life (good or had) demand recompense in the next or in future existences. The Norns water the tree daily from their well and the drops trickling from the tree provide food for all, i.e. destiny affects all. Reference to bees and honey means that destiny brings about metamorphosis. The presence of swans signifies the possibility of higher development.*

*Head, heart and limbs: thinking, feeling and willing are here portrayed.*

*The eagle in the treetop represents consciousness and the falcon that consciousness appertaining to the world of the senses. The squirrel and his up-and-down activity characterises the struggle between the awakened head organisation and the regions of passion, the struggle between higher and lower impulses. The stags eating the buds symbolise astral forces which destoy the life forces.*

*The human being, the tree, contains faculties not yet developed but which will manifest in the course of time.*

## Asgard, the Home of the Gods

Asgard was the home of the Aesir. There was one hall in Asgard where the Aesir sometimes met which was called Gladsheim (the Home of Joy) but when they had to make important decisions regarding the fate of human beings, they met at the well of Urd.

Odin was the foremost among the Aesir. He had his own special hall known as Valhalla, the Hall of the Chosen Slain. Spears lined the walls; golden shields, the roof. When a great battle had been fought on earth, Odin sent his Battle Maidens, the Valkyrs, to bring back the chosen heroes, i.e. those who had died but had proved themselves bold and brave. In Valhalla they feasted and waged desperate fights with one another but when the horn sounded for dinner, all wounds were healed. There they would live until the Day of Ragnarok when all things would end and all begin anew.

Odin had many names. He was 'Allfather', 'The Wanderer', 'The Traveller', 'The One who Knows', according to what he was doing and where he was. Two wolves accompanied him. He had a high seat in Asgard from where he could look out over the whole world. On his shoulders perched two ravens who kept him informed of all that was taking place.

Odin's wife was Frigga, the daughter of one of the older gods, the Vanir. She shared Odin's power and dignity.

The children of Odin and Frigga had their own halls or palaces. There were twelve in all.

Thor was the youngest and the most powerful. His wife was the goldenhaired Sif. Thor fought continually against the evil giants and all those who wished to destroy the rule of the gods. He had a girdle of strength and, when he wore it, he could wade through water which never rose higher than his middle. The girdle also doubled his power. He had a magic hammer called Mjölnir (the Crusher) which the giants feared. He could throw it and smash anything it hit, then it returned to his hand. He also had a pair of iron gloves which he wore when going out to battle. His chariot was pulled by two goats.

Thor's estate was called Thrudwang, the 'Meadow of the Brave'. His hall was Bilskirne, which means 'clear weather'.

Thor was the protector of the common people. He was not concerned with rank but looked for each individual's own qualities of strength and bravery. He was the patron of the farming freeman. When it thundered and lightened, the Norse people believed that Thor was riding out.

The most loved of the gods was Balder, Balder the Beautiful, and his wife, Nanna. His face was like the bright day. He was ever friendly, never spoke evil and no-one ever spoke evil of him. As well as spreading an aura of joy and light, Balder was also wise. As long as Balder lived men could talk with gods but evil times came . . . .

Balder's hall was Breidablick, which means 'a wide view' and it was the most beautiful in Asgard. He had a son, Forseti the just.

Tyr was the god of war, the bravest of the gods. Nordic people called on him for help when they went into battle. He carried a sword in his left hand because an adventure—still to be told—had cost him his right.

Another son of Odin was Bragi, musician and poet. His wife was Iduna, the keeper of the golden apples. These gave the gods their forces of rejuvenation. When old age threatened, the apples made them young again.

Hoder was the blind son of Odin; Ull, the god of archery and ski-ing. Vidar was called 'the Silent One'. He served the others.

In the ranks of the gods Heimdall had a special place. He guarded the rainbow bridge and sounded his horn for all the world to hear at the day of doom. He was said to be the son of nine mothers. Both day and night he could see movement a hundred leagues away. He slept less than a bird and he could hear the sound of grass growing and also the wool growing on a sheep's back. His hall was Himinbjorg which means 'cliffs of heaven'.

There were other gods in Asgard. One was Loki, the trickster, about whom many stories have to be told. He was a distant relative of Odin's and so claimed the right to live there. Njord and his children, Frey and Freya, also lived in Asgard and other stories will tell how they came there but the following can be said about them now.

Njord had power over wind, wave and fire. He was rich and could give his friends fine gifts from land and sea. Frey ruled over the changing weather, the rain and the sunshine, the growth in the fields and he also influenced human desires. Work in the house and fields succeeded with the blessing of Frey. He had a sword which fought by itself and a wonderful ship called Skidbladnir. Frey could travel through the air on this ship.

Freya was his sister, the most beautiful of the gods. She had a wonderful necklace called the Brising necklace, named after a race of dwarfs and, because of this treasure, she also had another name—Menglad which means 'happy with the necklace'.

*Spiritual science teaches us about higher beings who dwell in spiritual regions, but the knowledge is not new. Primitive peoples and past civilisations have all had their 'gods'. What is different is the understanding of them and the nomenclature.*

*In the Bible we find the names of many of the higher beings—Angels, Archangels, Principalities, Powers, Dominions, Cherubim, Seraphim. They have different ranks and different functions. They work from different regions.*

*Dr. Steiner tells us that the clairvoyant consciousness of the Norse peoples stretched to the experience of angels and archangels. These were their 'gods', the so-called Aesir, who led the races and educated them. They were beings who were concerned with the awakening of the individual human ego. They knew that eating from the Tree of Knowledge was a necessary step in evolution. History shows the development of individual consciousness from group consciousness and the Nordic-Germanic peoples experienced the beings who gave them psychic potentialities and ego-consciousness. The gifts of Odin, Honir and Lodur were already mentioned.*

*It is the task of the angel to guide individuals. It is the task of the archangel to guide the race. The archangels are in the strictest sense the folk-spirits of the peoples. They work within a certain area and with a certain people.*

*To think of higher worlds without thinking of them spatially is difficult. To our minds heaven is above and hell below although of course they exist in an entirely different dimension. Similarly, the Nordic-Germanic peoples imagined their gods in a particular location and with their own dwellings. They called it Asgard, the realm of the Aesir, and it was connected to Midgard by a rainbow bridge, guarded by Heimdall, the watchman.*

*In the Bible story of the Flood a rainbow appears for the first time in history. Seeing the colours of the rainbow signifies a change of perception. The world of the senses is developing and clairvoyance, i.e. living with the gods, is fading.*

*In the Norse version the gods withdraw to their own realm. Heaven and earth are now separate entities but the rainbow forms a connecting link. The Aesir can ride over the bridge to Midgard but no person crosses the bridge in the other direction. Midgard, the physical world, was the home created for humans.*

*The rainbow bridge must be guarded so that humanity can develop in Midgard, the new earth, where awareness awakens to the physical world and where new evolutionary forces of thinking and sense perception develop. The giants, of course, i.e. retarding forces, would like to storm Asgard from where the new inspiration comes but it is Heimdall's task to prevent them.*

*As the spiritual beings in higher worlds work from the different directions of the cosmos, so the Nordic peoples experienced their gods living in different 'halls'.*

*Odin had the famous Hall of the Slain, Valhalla, but Odin also has a high seat in Asgard from where he can survey the world. His two ravens symbolise the Power of thinking and the power of spiritual recollection. His wife, Frigga, represents Mother Earth.*

*In his book on karmic relationships Rudolf Steiner describes the work of the Archangel Michael in the spiritual world as collecting and educating particular souls for a future mission on earth. The same idea applies to Valhalla. Those slain in battle have not used up their life forces and these forces stream back into the race. The Valkyrs are the guardian angels. They bring back to the spiritual world those who have died and selected souls are educated by Odin for a future mission.*

*Odin has many names because he fulfills many roles or because they accord with his many deeds. In his role as the greatest authority he is called Allfather. He is known to various peoples, each of which give him their own name. His task is to awaken the forces of thought, to activate soul life, to develop intellect. It is his continued activity which causes Balder to have had dreams.*

*Thor is characterised as a rough, rumbustious, hearty fellow with a red beard and an enormous appetite. It is difficult to imagine him, as Dr. Steiner suggests, as an angel figure. However, he is obviously closely connected to the single human being and the 'folksy' stories which are told about him show with what deep affection he was held. He is the intermediary between the Folk Spirit and the individual. The Nordic peoples experienced the birth of ego-consciousness as Thor's influence. They felt the pulsation of the blood as the striking of the hammer. The heartbeat is connected with the blood circulation; the heart forces with courage. Thor is a choleric, full of will and life forces.*

*When he throws his hammer, it returns to him. This is a picture of the blood flowing to the extremities and back again. Thor has to cross rivers in his journeyings; again a picture of the flowing blood.*

*In blood is iron, hence the symbolism of the hammer made of iron and the iron gloves. Thor is often angry, He 'gets his blood up'. Ego forces are his. His task is to protect, to establish order. He is forever engaged in a struggle with the giants. This is a picture of ego forces asserting themselves against powers of a bygone age which would hinder man's development. The ego is the human being's most recent acquisition, hence Thor is Odin's youngest son.*

*Thor has a girdle of strength, i.e. the support of the macrocosm. His chariot is drawn by two goats, symbols of the search for earthly knowledge.*

*As a storm within clears the soul, so a storm without clears the atmosphere; hence the belief that Thor manifested in thunder and lightning.*

*Thor is married to Sif. Sif is cognate with Sippe, the German word meaning a tribe. Sif represents the group soul. The experience of ego was first felt in the group, then it becomes individualised. It is Thor's task to promote this.*

*In Balder is represented the experience of clairvoyant consciousness. In the tragedy of his death is the loss of spiritual vision. His bad dreams were due to this approaching loss. His influence was a healing one. (It is interesting to note that the Chamomile was known at one time in Germany as Balder's brow. The Chamomile has light and warmth in strong concentration and is effective against inflammations.)*

*Bragi, poet and musician, is inspired by his wife, Iduna. Her apples represent the forces in the human soul which may still commune with the gods. Her love to Bragi gives him wings of inspiration.*

*Hoder, the blind god, represents the physical entirely cut off from the spiritual. When nature is conquered through the intellect, spiritual vision disappears.*

*Vidar is the most enigmatical figure. It is he who eventually overcomes the power that overcomes Odin. He is a survivor and a re-creator. His is the future. In Asgard, he is 'the Silent One' and servant of others.*

*Heimdall is characterised as having extremely well-developed earthly senses. The nine mothers would refer to the nine muses, i.e. he is a figure of great wisdom and importance. In an earthly context he would be a high initiate; otherwise a high-ranking spiritual being.*

*Loki is the Nordic Lucifer, the fallen angel; hence he can claim relationship with Odin. His role becomes clear in the many stories told about him.*

*Njord, Frey and Freya have a story for themselves.*

*In most versions of the Nordic mythology Mimir is described as a giant. He is, however, a very different figure and his role is clearer if he is not associated with them, hence he has here the appellation of the Ancient One. His significance was mentioned in the Creation story and he, too, appears again in other stories.*

## The Lay of Loddfafnir

Midgard was the region allotted to human beings. They were helped and educated in various ways both by gods and humans inspired by the gods. One such learned teacher was called Loddfafnir which means 'Dragon-slayer'.

One evening Loddfafnir was the guest at a gathering of men and women in a farmhouse. He spoke to them and explained how he had sat in the High One's Hall and had listened to the runes; now he would repeat what he had heard.

"Be careful in getting up at night. Look out for witches and pay no heed to their promises. Do not seduce another man's wife. Take enough food for journeys. Trust no evil man. Seek a wise one and learn his charms for healing. Use no angry words. Do not take part in wickedness. Keep your promises. Mock no-one. Do not despise the old. Be generous. Use like to cure like in sickness."

"These words are for the good of men and the curse of giants."

*Loddfafnir means 'Dragon-slayer'. To slay the dragon (of one's own lower impulses) is the first step to initiation. This 'lay' is a path of instruction.*

*In earlier times the soul could easily be influenced by the dark beings of the night; hence care is needed. Neophytes have to guard against the influence of evil powers; they have to overcome their own lower passions and urges; they have to differentiate between good and evil, recognise what is good and act positively. Furthermore, they are advised to use the homoeopathic way of healing. The ego forces must become strong.*

## How Odin gained Wisdom

In order to help the people of Midgard, Odin sought to obtain wisdom, even if this meant hardship and sacrifice on his part.

One day he sought out Mimir and asked for a draught of water from his well but the Ancient One refused, saying that he alone, or those of his race, might drink from it. Odin persisted and offered to pay any price for it. Never thinking that his visitor would agree, the Ancient One suggested an eye. Immediately Odin plucked out an eye and handed it over, receiving a horn of the precious liquid in exchange. He drank it and it gave him great wisdom, the knowledge of that wisdom that lives in the sounds of speech.

The eye was placed at the bottom of the well. The water became more powerful and, in drinking it, Mimir's wisdom increased even more.

Another time Odin caused himself to be hung for nine days and nights in the high branches of Yggdrasil, the world Tree. No-one brought him food or wine. He was pierced by a spear. He felt himself carried away into higher realms where he learned many secrets. He learned that the world and human beings were formed through the magic power of the divine word and that he himself could use the power of the word to heal, to quench fires, to thwart evil and to calm stormy weather.

He realised that, to teach human beings the use of the word, he would have to obtain the Mead of Poetry. How he did this is told in the story of Kvasir.

When the nine days were accomplished, Mimir released him, reminded him of all he had experienced and became his teacher.

*The Nordic peoples designated Odin 'The Lord of the Power of Language', the 'Master of the Runes', and looked upon him as the creator of speech. They experienced him in the element of air, in the winds outside, in the breath within. When Odin gains wisdom, it is essentially a matter of his gaining knowledge of speech and language. There are three stages and three stories but it is difficult to bring them into any logical sequence since the events interweave.*

*One story says that through the sacrifice of his eye Odin gained a drink from Mimir's well. Another says he received the draught while hanging on the World Tree. There is also mention of his drinking of the Mead of Poetry on the tree although this is a separate story and it is said that he had no refreshment there.*

*It is also difficult to know whether we are dealing with Odin as a purely spiritual being, whether his exploits are put in human context or whether we consider him as an incarnated initiate.*

*Odin had given soul to the human being. To have a soul means to have an inner life. The Aesir are concerned with human development to ego-consciousness. The next stage on this path is for the soul to have the means of expressing itself. Speech is the medium. Odin is therefore concerned with giving human beings the power of speech. To do this he must acquire new powers, powers which are related to human understanding. This required sacrifice on his part.*

*According to Rudolf Steiner this sacrifice consisted in his giving up advancement to higher rank in the spiritual world. It is put in symbolic form by the giving up of his eye.*

*In the story as we have it, Odin gives up his eye at Mimir's well in exchange for wisdom. (This, in itself, is a reflection of human evolution. Insofar as gods and humans develop together the significance of this act is that humanity loses clairvoyant perception. It is in the plan of evolution that clairvoyance shall fade in favour of learning through the senses. This is part of a step towards independence which can only come about when direct connection with the gods is broken.)*

*Mimir is reluctant to part with the water and, from his point of view, rightly so. He is keeper of the world memory and must preserve what is holy but he does not know the future where apparently 'unholy' things must happen.*

*The sacrifice which Odin makes adds to Mimir's capacities which, in turn, assist Odin. It is said that the eye lies at the bottom of the well and Mimir drinks daily from the water, whereby he becomes wiser.*

*The new wisdom which Odin gains is connected with speech. Drinking the water from Mimir's well, the well of remembrance, signifies an initiation. Odin learns the mysteries of creation through the divine word. He learns that the word has creative power and that he himself can use this power. He gains knowledge of the wisdom that lives in the sound of the spoken word.*

*The story of his hanging in the tree represents a further initiation. 'Hanging in the Tree' signifies a sojourn in a higher world. Suffering and hardship bring knowledge. Odin learns to use the power which lives in speech. Human speech is carried on the breath. Breath must be drawn into the body for speech to be carried out on it. This he experiences as the spear.*

*The fact that while in the tree he already speaks of the Mead of Poetry (the content of another story, Kvasir) may be a preview of events to come.*

*The clairvoyant person of Atlantean times experienced the hidden tones resounding in nature. He or she was gifted with great powers of memory. Remembering and repeating tones led to the development of speech. It was Odin's task to influence human development in such a way that these tones could become consciously formed speech.*

## The War between Aesir and Vanir

A race of gods older than the Aesir was that of the Vanir. Their home was a region far above the top of Yggdrasil. They worked in everything that grows and lives, in the wind, in the warmth, in sprouting seeds, in the rising sap of the trees and, of course, in humankind as well. But the Aesir worked in human thinking, feeling and willing.

A visitor from the Vanir, called Gullveig, once came to Asgard but talked of nothing but the golden age. The Aesir thought she wanted to hinder them in their work and tried to get rid of her. This proved impossible. They threw her on a fire three times and she burned up three times but three times she became alive again. Loki ate some of her burnt heart. Gullveig, resurrected however, stayed in Asgard, changed her name to Heid and became a witch.

The Vanir were angry at the way their messenger had been insulted and swore vengeance. Thus a war started but it soon became clear that no one side would win and, growing weary, the two contestants called a truce. They made peace and exchanged hostages. Njord and Heimdall came to live in Asgard and were soon accepted as Aesir.

Honir and Mimir went to Vanaheim but the Vanir were not pleased with their guests. Honir never seemed able to answer a question properly and always said, "Ask Mimir." The Vanir realised that Mimir was not a real member of the Aesir and they began to look upon him as a sorcerer. They felt they had been tricked. They cut off his head and sent it back to Asgard. Odin smeared it with herbs to preserve it and sang charms over it so that the power of speech came back to it. So Mimir's wisdom became Odin's.

*The Vanir were the gods active in distant Atlantean times before other gods intervened in the soul nature of the human being. The war between Aesir and Vanir represents conflicting interests concerning the future of humans. The Vanir are deities concerned with cosmic rhythms to which humans are exposed but which affect them subconsciously. The Aesir are concered with the souls of human beings and their coming to self-consciousness.*

*The visitor represents former supersensible forces and when she talks of a golden age, it is the age of innocence, before the Fall. Since, however, she now brings forces of an earlier time which are not transmuted and therefore are no longer appropriate, she becomes a witch. When Loki partakes of her flesh it signifies that he can misuse supersensible powers. The visit marks the end of the golden age, historically.*

*The Aesir lead humanity from dependence on the gods to independence and the way leads through contact with the physical world. They, therefore, have no patience with one who continually talks of times past. There is conflict but gods also evolve and there is eventual agreement. Hostages are exchanged. The significance of this is that there is now a working together. The fact that Njord leaves Vanaheim means that there is to be a change in the manner of reproduction. Njord represents the reproductive forces which are now to be governed by different conditions.*

*In the golden age there was no conscious sexuality. Conception took place in a somnambulistic state under divine influence and hence one could say of a woman that "she knew not a man." People lived in accord with cosmic rhythms and, as with most animals today, conception only took place at certain times. The urge to reproduce is to come no longer from without but from within. It becomes a conscious act as Njord comes to live in Asgard.*

*Heimdall was already mentioned as a high ranking spiritual being, who, although a member of the Vanir, worked in the sense world. He had obviously changed his nature and could therefore be at home in Asgard.*

*Honir and Mimir go to Vanaheim, the home of the Vanir. Honir, who had given the first man and woman a mind, represents a part of the human being which was withdrawn from entanglement with the senses, the higher self, which is preserved for the advent of a new spiritual impulse later. He was 'innocent' and hence could not answer questions properly.*

*Mimir, as bearer of the world memory, is at home in any realm and was therefore no real hostage. When humanity loses spiritual vision, the event is described as if the gods have withdrawn. Similarly, Mimir, cosmic memory, spiritual perception, recedes further from the earthly world.*

*When the Vanir cut off Mimir's head, it is the Norse way of saying that cosmic memory is no longer available to humans; they lose contact with the spiritual world. Nevertheless, cosmic reality still exists and Odin 'embalmed' this. The head was able to speak to Odin, that is to say, Odin had the faculty of understanding. He had learned cosmic language.*

## Kvasir and the Magic Mead

The end of the war between the Vanir and the Aesir was celebrated by a great feast. Not only did they exchange hostages but, to put a seal on their peace-making, everyone of them spit into a great jar. Out of their spittle the Aesir formed a man. He was called Kvasir and because he had received something from so many, his wisdom was inexhaustible. He became a poet.

Stories of Kvasir's wisdom reached the ears of the wicked dwarfs, Fjalar and Galar. They invited Kvasir to visit them and advise them. Then they murdered him. They mixed honey with his blood and so prepared a magic mead which had the power of making anyone who drank it a poet.

One day the dwarfs invited a giant and his wife to visit them. They quarrelled and eventually the dwarfs arranged things that the giant was drowned and his wife killed by a displaced rock. But the giants had a son, Suttung, who was suspicious about his parents' disappearance. He threatened to drown the two dwarfs if they did not tell the truth. They were so frightened that they admitted the deed and offered him the magic mead in recompense. Suttung took the mead to a cave in the mountains and set his daughter, Gunnlod, to guard it.

Unlike the dwarfs, Suttung boasted about his treasure and Odin learned about it. He decided that, in the interests of men, he must acquire it. Disguised as a labourer, Odin came to the lands on the edge of Jotunheim where Baugi, the brother of Suttung, lived. He found nine men mowing and asked them how they liked working for a giant. They said that they had problems in keeping their scythes sharp. The labourer drew a whetstone from his belt and offered to sharpen them. The effect was so astounding that they wanted to buy the whetstone. Odin threw it in the air for the best man to get but in the confusion the workmen killed one another. Odin picked the stone up and went on his way.

He came to Baugi's house and Baugi complained about the loss of his labourers and hence the failure to harvest his crops. Odin offered to do the work in return for Baugi's help in obtaining Suttung's mead. This was agreed. Odin completed the harvesting and Baugi asked his brother for a horn of the mead. The request was in vain.

Odin asked to be taken to the mountain in which the mead was stored. He took an augur from his pocket and told Baugi to drill a hole. When it was done, Odin turned himself into a snake and slipped through. He crawled into the treasure chamber and turned himself into a handsome young giant. Gunnlod was pleased and could not resist the advances of the handsome newcomer. She was so in love that when he asked for a drink of the mead she gave it to him immediately. There were three vessels full and he emptied them all. Then he asked to see the sky but as soon as Gunnlod opened a door at the top of a shaft of rock, Odin turned himself into an eagle and flew away.

Sultung saw him and realised what had happened. He turned himself also into an eagle and gave chase. Meanwhile the Aesir were waiting on the walls of Asgard. They saw two eagles flying towards them, one close behind the other. They placed golden vessels in the courtyard. The first eagle dived over the wall and spat the mead of inspiration into the waiting vessels and, in a flash of light, Odin stood there again. The second eagle shrieked and wheeled away.

The Aesir drank of the mead and gave it to the dwellers of Midgard. Whoever drank of it became a poet.

Odin had had difficulty in holding all the mead and some passed through him and fell outside the wall. Whoever drank of that could only compose inferior verse.

*In the period of the Vanir the forces of speech and reproduction were closely related. In the course of evolution physical changes took place in the human constitution. Human souls and bodies became less pliable. Speech developed through the larynx and reproduction through the sex organs. (The fact that these organs are connected is illustrated by the change of voice in the male at puberty.)*

*This story is connected with the development of the larynx.*

*After the war between Vanir and Aesir, all the gods spit into a jar. In spittle there are healing forces and this, then, is a sign of conciliation. But spittle is connected with speech. It is impossible to speak with a dry mouth and when the gods spit, it signifies that divine powers are at work on the formation of the organs of speech. Kvasir is the product of many divine throats. Becoming a poet signifies the ability to speak.*

*Kvasir is not a character as such but represents the power of primeval speech which created and united all things. Hence he is a token of peace.*

*The art of speaking belongs to the ego-endowed human being. The Aesir are the gods who bring men and women to self-consciousness and give them the ability to express themselves. This is a part of ego development. The Aesir create Kvasir. He embodies what Odin had learnt at Mimir's well and on the tree.*

*Evil forces, which we should describe as Ahrimanic (characterised in the story of The Building of Asgard's Wall), are at work. Their object is to frustrate the aims of the gods and gain power for themselves. Hence the picture of the dwarfs murdering Kvasir and mixing his blood with honey. Honey symbolises a process of metamorphosis. Thus the magic mead is prepared.*

*So the power of speech as the gods had intended it is transformed. Instead of Kvasir there is the mead made from his blood. Language has lost its creative ability; it becomes an abstraction, a means of communication, a shell. Henceforth the universal nature of language is lost and there will be confusion and estrangement among men. The mead is tainted.*

*Yet this lies within the destiny of humankind and Odin cannot distance himself from it. Retarding forces, in the shape of Suttung, try to hold back evolution and Odin has to overcome them. The way he does this echoes an initiation process—trials to be overcome, guise of a snake (a symbol of the initiate), penetration into a mountain, three days sojourn and escape as an eagle.*

*So Odin brings the mead to Asgard. The Aesir give it to human beings. They receive the gift of speech and the larynx has become its instrument.*

## The Apples of Iduna

Once a boat came sailing towards Midgard and a youth playing a golden harp stepped out of it. The Aesir heard the music and crossed the rainbow bridge to meel the minstrel. Before they met, the earth opened and out stepped a beautiful maiden, the daughter of Ivaldi the dwarf, holding a casket of gold full of rosy apples. The minstrel took her hand and they walked together towards the Aesir. As they met, the minstrel spoke: "Greetings, Lords of Asgard. Though I come from Jotunheim, I am one of yourselves for Odin is my father. My name is Bragi. My mother is Gunnlod, the former keeper of the magic mead. I come to sing and play for you. This is my bride, Iduna, bringing the Apples of Youth."

So Bragi and Iduna settled among the Aesir and Iduna gave her apples to them. However many she gave away the casket remained full and the Aesir remained young.

*The cosmic creative word has already been mentioned but not the fact that this 'word' was not pure speech but a sort of song-speech.*

*Odin brings the magic mead of speech to Asgard after his encounter with Gunniod. Bragi is the result of his association with her, i.e. his son, and what Bragi brings is really the other half of the song-speech.*

*Iduna is described as a daughter of Ivaldi by his first wife, the sun goddess. (Later Ivaldi married a giantess and the children of that union came under the influence of Loki.) Thus Iduna is a product of sun and earth forces but arising out of the earth expresses innocence. Hence Iduna can be looked upon as representing the uncontaminated soul forces which have a direct connection with the divine. The manifestation of these forces appears as beauty, art or music, Her apples are spiritual nourishment.*

*Iduna's love for Bragi lends him wings of inspiration; i.e. he creates from a spiritual source.*

## The Theft of Iduna's Apples

One day, Odin, Honir and Loki were visiting Midgard to observe the ways of mortal men. Feeling hungry, they killed an ox and tried to roast it. However, the meat would not cook and they realised that some magic was at work. A voice above them spoke. It was an eagle. "Agree that I can first eat my fill and the meat will cook," said the eagle. The gods assented.

Soon the meat was ready. The eagle swooped down and it seemed as if it would consume the lot. Loki grew angry and struck the bird with a stick but the stick stuck to its feathers and the eagle flew off with Loki hanging onto the stick. He was dragged over sharp stones and rocks, through trees and bushes and feared for his life. The eagle explained that the ox was his and that the visitors were trespassing but that Loki could go free if he would promise to bring him Iduna and her apples.

Now Loki realised that the eagle was the giant, Thiassi, in disguise. He was frightened but promised to do his best and the eagle released him. He returned to Odin and Honir but said nothing about the giant and his promise. They all went back to Asgard.

Mindful of his promise to Thiassi, Loki sought his opportunity. On one occasion he came across Iduna playing with her apples and he told her that he had seen better apples growing in a little wood not very far away. Iduna was curious and allowed herself to be taken thither. Thiassi, in his eagle form, was waiting. He swooped down and carried Iduna away.

Soon the Aesir began to wonder what had happened to Iduna. They missed her apples and began to look old and worn. Then Odin's raven found where she was held captive and the Aesir learned how Loki had been involved. They ordered him to bring her back.

Loki borrowed Freya's falcon skin and flew to Jotunheim, where he found Iduna shut up in a tower. By his magic he turned her into a nut, seized the nut in his claws and flew off. Thiassi had been out fishing and when he returned, he realised what had happened. Donning his eagle dress he went off in pursuit.

From the walls of Asgard the Aesir could see a falcon approaching, pursued and being overtaken by a great eagle. They put bundles of woodshavings on the battlements and, as the falcon soared over the walls, lit them. The eagle could not stop or turn and flew into the fire, crashing inside Asgard. The Aesir killed him there. This brought trouble to them later because the place was sacred and no-one should be killed on holy ground.

Loki threw off the falcon skin, spoke the magic words and there stood Iduna again with her apples of youth.

*It is the aim of the giants, the powers of a bygone age, to hinder human progress, i.e. they would keep humanity in the old stage of dream-consciousness. Thiassi represents such a retarding force. The Aesir need Iduna and her apples because they represent spiritual refreshment; they give the Aesir the strength to carry out their task of leading man to ego-consciouness.*

*Thiassi sets a trap. Soul forces, in the shape of Odin, Honir and Loki, seek nourishment in earthly experience but the earthly substance, the ox, is infected. Thiassi appears in the form of an eagle and suggests a pact but pacts made with powers of evil exact a price and even so may not be honoured. The meat is cooked but the gods get none of it.*

*Passions are roused in the form of Loki's getting cross but passions lead to chaos and entanglement as Loki finds out. He has to extricate himself by involving Iduna, i.e. by giving away the food of the gods, which was what Thiassi desired.*

*Loki abducts her and hands her over to Thiassi. It is a picture of innocent forces being overwhelmed through passion.*

*When the Aesir realise that Iduna is missing, it is an experience of the soul awakening.*

*Loki dons a falcon cloak, representing thinking forces which overcome instincts. The rejuvenating forces are restored but at a cost. In Asgard the eagle crashes into the ego fire of the Aesir, but evil forces come by this means into Asgard. Although the apples are returned, the Aesir have experienced an ageing process. It is a foretaste of the Götterdämmerung, the Twilight of the Gods.*

## The Marriage of Njord and Skadi

On learning of the death of Thiassi, his daughter, Skadi, came to the Aesir to demand compensation. The Aesir knew that they had brought trouble upon themselves by killing on holy ground and they agreed to what she asked for. This was that one of the Aesir should become her husband and that someone should make her laugh.

Odin stipulated that she must choose her future husband by his feet and accordingly the male Aesir showed her their feet only. She chose those she considered the most beautiful, thinking that these must belong to Balder. In fact, however, they were Njord's. Nevertheless, they both seemed contented. Loki made her laugh by playing tricks with a goat and the wedding was celebrated. (Loki put the loop of a rope round his testicles and tied the other end to a goat's beard. Then they had a tug of war.) As a goodwill gesture Odin took two marbles from his pocket—they were Thiassi's eyes—and hurled them into the sky where they became stars. Njord and Skadi had two children, Frey and Freya, who were accepted as Aesir.

The marriage was, however, not a happy one. Njord wished to dwell by the sea where he could hear the crying of the swans. Skadi wanted to live among the mountains where she could hear the howling of the wolves. They agreed to spend nine nights together in each place but gradually each settled in his or her chosen home.

*When old powers are overcome or discarded, something new must develop. What develops here is in the realm of consciousness. The story is an echo of that of the Fall.*

*In a roundabout way it is due to Loki (Lucifer) that Skadi marries Njord. Through the death of her father she comes to Asgard to seek a husband but has to choose on the merit of feet. Feet have a special relationship with the earth and choosing by the feet means choosing one with this special relationship or, in this case, non-relationship. Njord belongs to the golden age, which was not yet connected with the physical earth, so he has beautiful feet, His was the time of unconscious sexuality as described earlier. Skadi belongs to Jotunheim, the symbolic region of material forces. The fact that she wants to laugh indicates a loosening of consolidating forces. Laughing is a human characteristic. Note the means by which it is achieved in this case.*

*It is due to Lucifer that man comes to physical incarnation (The Fall) and in Njord marrying Skadi is a picture of man coming to earth and the resultant changes in the conditions of reproduction. (In sorrow shalt thou bring forth children.)*

*Dwelling by the sea and in the mountains characterises the two marriage partners. The sea and the swans indicate the non-material; the mountains and the wolves, the very essence of materialism.*

*The changing of Thiassi's eyes into stars indicates also the changing consciousness. The dream state becomes one of clear perception by the senses.*

# The Building of Asgard's Wall

One day a figure on horseback, representing himself as a master-builder, came riding over the rainbow bridge to Asgard. He was stopped by Heimdall, the watchman, who then arranged for him to meet the Aesir as requested. The stranger offered to build a wall around Asgard for the protection of the Aesir. He said he would do it in eighteen months but his price was Freya for a wife, the sun and the moon.

No-one would agree but Loki suggested that they should think it over and the stranger left. Loki advised that they should narrow the time limit to six months and when the builder returned, he was offered these terms. He agreed on condition that he could have his horse, a stallion, to help him. Loki advised acceptance.Soon the wall began to take shape and it locked as if the contract would be finished in time but the Aesir got anxious and threatened Loki with death unless he found some way of frustrating the work.

A day or two before the six months were up, Loki changed himself into a frisky mare, danced in front of the builder's stallion and ran off into the woods. The stallion followed and try as he would, the builder could not get him back. Thus he failed to complete the work in time. He was in a great rage and burst out of his disguise to reveal himself as an evil giant. The Aesir called Thor, who had been away on a journey, and Thor killed him with his great hammer.

Loki was not seen for a long time and then he came back in his own form leading a colt with eight legs. He gave it to Odin and told him that this horse, Sleipnir, would outpace all others, could gallop over sea, land and through the air and even go into the land of the dead and come back again.

*Powers of evil have been recognised from time immemorial and they have a role to play in evolution. Furthermore, although designated 'powers of evil', their influence is by no means wholly so. They give the human race possibilities which it may not otherwise have. Only if human beings allow themselves to become dominated by them are they evil.*

*There are two opposite spirits of adversity, known as Luciferic and Ahrimanic. The former have the effect of making the human being independent; they offer choice, initiative, enthusiasm, freedom but at the same time passions and the possibility of doing wrong. They do not want to shut the human being off from the spiritual world but inspire self-seeking, self-aggrandisement, pride, ambition.*

*The Ahrimanic forces are those which lead to substantiality, to consolidation, to the idea that the material world is the only reality and that Paradise is of this world. They inspire a utilitarian, mechanistic view of the world and humanity, and dull human consciousness to the extent that spiritual vision is lost. Ahriman, as a figure-head, is known as the 'Father of Lies'.*

*These two powers each work for their own ends yet support one another. They would each like to take the leadership of humanity into their own hands and away from the progressive beings.*

*In the Bible is the story of the Fall through the influence of Lucifer. Adam and Eve are driven from Paradise after eating from the Tree of Knowledge. It is the beginning of terrestrial existence and ego-consciousness. Loki is the Nordic equivalent of Lucifer, the fallen angel, but the story is somewhat different. Loki had been accepted into the circle of the Aesir. The significance of this is that the Aesir knew that he had a role to play in evolution. In Norse mythology it is the gods themselves who experience the Fall, indeed they bring it about. With the acceptance of Loki, with the rejection of Gullveig, the Golden Age, the age of the Vanir, comes to an end.*

*Since Lucifer offers choice (between good and evil) other forces of evil can enter the field, namely, Ahriman. The building of Asgard's wall is a story of rivalry and co-operation between the two powers.*

*The Master-builder, revealing himself as a giant, represents Ahriman. He wishes to restrict the work of normal evolution, to gain control of the reproductive forces and cosmic rhythms. He has other ideas for human development and would wish the human being to be directed solely to the physical world. For the moment, Loki, always ready to confuse his fellows, co-operates and advises acceptance of the offer to build the wall.*

*The Aesir are of the opinion that there is no danger since the task of building the wall in the stipulated time seems impossible but they reckon without Ahriman's intellectual powers, symbolised by his horse. Loki-Lucifer, by whose advice the work was started, is now called upon to thwart its completion. It is not in his interest that Ahriman should dominate. Lucifer, a being who belongs to the element of fire, is one who can change his form and nature. He is the inspirer of passions which can grow and change. He becomes a mare and seduces the builder's stallion. Thus he brings it about that the wall remains unfinished.*

*When the builder is revealed in his true form, Thor, representing the developing ego force, despatches him.*

*The product of the union between Loki and the intellectual forces of the master-builder is Sleipnir which Loki gives to Odin. Sleipnir represents a balance of forces, enthusiasm combined with intellect, passion combined with reason. Loki provides Odin with the means of ranging freely over the whole world. One is reminded of Pegasus, the winged horse of Greek mythology—a symbol of the power of imagination or the ability to penetrate to higher spheres. This is a positive side of the Luciferic influence.*

*One could also look upon the events as taking place within the individual soul. There is co-operation and conflict between the two forces. There is the threat of being overwhelmed but the soul has a revelation and uses the positive side of the Luciferic forces. The ego conquers the forces of materialism. A balance is achieved which gives the possibility of attaining higher knowledge.*

## Loki's Children

At times Loki liked to wander off to other regions. In Jotunheim he met a giantess called Angurboda and fell in love with her. He married her and three children were born to them but they were monsters. The eldest was a wolf called Fenris; the second was the serpent, Jormungand and the youngest was Hela who had a body which consisted half of living flesh and the other half, decaying. They lived at first in Jotunheim.

Odin knew that it was fate that these three were born but he ordered Thor to bring them to him.

Hela he sent to live in a region below all others, to be Queen of the Dead and rule over those spirits of men who did not die in battle, those who were weak, and also those who were evil-doers.

Odin threw the serpent into the sea where it grew until it surrounded the whole of Midgard and held its tail in its mouth. There it was fated to stay until the day of Ragnarok.

The Fenris wolf was kept in Asgard where he grew and grew and grew. He became so fierce that the Aesir decided to tie him up but they knew that they could only do it by cunning. Accordingly they made a strong chain and challenged the Fenris wolf to be bound by it. He broke it easily. They made a stronger chain but he broke that also. The Aesir decided they must use other means. They sent to the Black Dwarfs and asked them to make a chain. The dwarfs made one, using the sound of a cat's footsteps, the roots of a mountain, the sinews of a bear, the breath of a fish, the beard of a woman and the spittle of a bird. When finished, it looked like a silver cord.

When the Aesir approached the wolf with this cord, he was suspicious and only agreed to be bound with it if one of the Aesir put a hand in his mouth. Tyr the Brave volunteered.

So Fenris was bound and the cord held. The Aesir rejoiced but not so Tyr, for the wolf snapped his teeth together and bit off Tyr's hand. The Fenris wolf was tied down to a rock and roared so loudly that Thor put a sword in his mouth with the guard in the lower jaw and the point in the upper. There he stayed until he broke out on the day of Ragnarok.

*Although at times the Luciferic influence is beneficial, it becomes evil when it oversteps its mark or when united with the Ahrimanic. The latter is what is portrayed in the story of the marriage between Loki and Angurboda. (Angurboda is the same word as the Persian Angromainu—forces of darkness, Ahriman).*

*Such an influence can affect the human being in various ways. It destroys the life forces and perception of truth. It poisons the life of the soul, bringing with it passions, base impulses and selfishness. It brings about bodily sickness and death. The Nordic peoples saw these qualities as objects, hence the Serpent, Fenris Wolf and Hela.*

| | |
|---|---|
| *The Serpent* | *Selfishness* |
| *Fenris Wolf* | *Falsehood, Untruth* |
| *Hela* | *Sickness and Death* |

*Thor is sent to fetch the monsters from Jotunheim, i.e. the ego force brings these powers to consciousness in the soul.*

*In the world order there has to be a place for evil-doers where they are confronted by their own deeds. The idea is common to many religions. In the Nordic tradition Loki's daughter Hela is appointed guardian of such a place. 'Hela' becomes the English word 'hell'.*

*These forces, or these monsters, have to be resisted or neutralised. Odin threw the serpent into the sea where it grew until it surrounded the whole of Midgard, that is, the human world. In an applied sense the human soul is surrounded by negative forces.*

*The wolf is always the symbol of the dark, materialistic, hardening forces which dull the human consciousness. Being devoured by the wolf means the loss of spiritual vision which reaches its final stage on the day of Ragnarok. It is a step in the divine plan as the human being progresses towards freedom but there must also be a possibility of resurrection. Attempts must be made at redemption. Hence the wolf is kept in Asgard where the Aesir try to keep him in bounds. Tyr, the war god, looks after him. Only when his power goes beyond a certain limit must drastic steps be taken. Higher supernatural powers are invoked. The evil is contained but at a sacrifice. Tyr loses his hand. On the day of Ragnarok the Fenris wolf breaks loose.*

## The Treasures of the Gods

Loki was cross with Thor because the latter had fetched his children from Jotunheim and he was determined to take revenge.

He stole into the bedroom of Sif, Thor's wife, and, while she was asleep, cut off her golden hair. Thor was furious when he found out about it and threatened to break every bone in Loki's body if he did not replace it.

Loki went to the land of the black dwarfs and came to the cave of the sons of Ivaldi. He made a bargain with them that, if they produced golden hair which would grow on Sif's head and gave it to him, he would be at their service if ever they needed him.

The dwarfs made the hair in their furnace but, as it was already working, Loki suggested that they could win the favour of the gods by making them gifts. They made a ship called Skidbladnir which could sail over land and water and which could expand to fill the whole heavens but shrink small enough to put in a purse. They also made a spear called Gungnir which would never miss its mark.

Loki took the gifts but on the way back to Asgard he had a mischievous idea and called in at the hall of the dwarfs, Brock and Sindri. He showed them the gifts and made a bet with them of his head that they could not make better objects.

They took up the challenge. Sindri picked up a piece of pigskin and some pieces of gold wire and put them in the furnace, telling Brock to pump the bellows and not stop until told. A fly stung him on the hand but he kept pumping. In this way, Gullinbursti, the boar with bristles of gold, was created. He was an animal who could shine in the dark and fertilise all the land.

Sindri took a piece of gold, put it in the furnace and again told Brock to keep pumping. The same fly stung Brock in the throat but he kept pumping. Finally Sindri drew out a ring of gold, called Draupnir, from which would drop eight similar rings every ninth night.

Now Sindri put a great piece of iron in the furnace, repeated his instructions and began to work. The same fly stung Brock between the eyes. The blood blinded him for a moment and he paused to brush the fly away.

Some say the fly was Loki but more likely it was a rival.

Sindri drew a hammer from the furnace but the interruption had caused it to be a little short in the handle. He called it 'Mjölnir' (the Crusher).

He told Brock to go with Loki to Asgard and to take the treasures with him that the Aesir might decide which objects were the best.

On returning to Asgard Loki immediately gave Sif the hair which grew on her head again as if natural. He gave Skidbladnir to Frey; Gungnir, the spear, to Odin. Brock gave the boar to Frey, the ring to Odin and the hammer to Thor.

Then came the judgement as to which group of dwarfs had produced the finest objects.

The hammer was considered the most wonderful and magic instrument for combatting the giants and the gods decided that Sindri and Brock were the winners.

Brock immediately claimed Loki's head but Loki fled. Thor went after him and brought him back. Then Loki agreed that his head was forfeit but declared that his neck must not be damaged. Brock saw that he was outwitted but he took a leather thong from his pocket and sewed up Loki's lips. He, however, ran off and ripped off the thong with great pain, swearing vengeance. Loki had a twisted mouth ever since.

*The story deals with the Luciferic influence (the Fall in the Bible) which brought the human being into physical existence and to consciousness of self as an individual earlier than the creator gods had intended. The result was separation from the divine, division into races, different languages and dissension.*

*As in the fairy stories, golden hair signifies innocent wisdom, direct connection with the divine. When Sif's golden hair is replaced by that manufactured by the dwarfs, it symbolises replacement of heavenly wisdom by that of the earth.*

*There is a further connotation. Sif is cognate with the archaic English word 'Sib', meaning kindred, which we still have in 'sibling'. Thor represents the ego power. The union of Thor and Sif therefore signifies group consciousness, a group ego. When Sif loses her golden hair, it is the equivalent of the dissolution of group consciousness.*

*In place of the group consciousness, that of the individual develops. The gifts Loki persuades the dwarfs to make are for this purpose. Besides Sif's hair they make a magic ship and a spear. The magic ship symbolises the alternation of day and night, expansion and contraction, consciousness and unconsciousness. In earlier times the differentiation between sleeping and waking did not exist. The spear is the spear of speech, carried on the breath and fired by the will. Speech belongs to the ego-endowed human being.*

*These gifts then are directly inspired by Lucifer and are connected with forces which live in the soul; but where Lucifer opens the way, other forces which we have characterised as Ahrimanic can enter. Loki's interest is in creating discord.*

*Other dwarfs, Sindri and Brock, are prevailed upon to make gifts by way of competition. One of their creations is Gullinbursti, the boar which fertilises the land. Another is Draupnir, a ring from which eight other rings drop on the ninth night. The third is Mjölnir, the hammer. These are connected with the life forces, but in their creation there was a disturbance, hence they are tainted.*

*The boar with its golden bristles is a power with a high potential and essentially an earthy animal. The gift points in the direction of the physical world.*

*A ring has no beginning and no ending. It is complete in itself. Being able to reproduce itself means continuity but it must also have another significance. From the fact that the fly stung Brock in the throat we could deduce that the ring is connected with speech.*

*Mjölnir, the hammer, is symbolic of the heartbeat in the circulation of the blood. The hammer is made of iron. Blood is red when it has the necessary iron content. It circulates and comes back to its starting point.*

*In the manufacture of these three, the boar, the ring and the hammer, a fly on the wall tried to interrupt. This is obviously some negative influence. The story says Loki was the fly but one might suspect that it was his counterpart, an Ahrimanic being since Loki's sphere is the astral and these three gifts are connected with the life force.*

*When making the boar, Brock was stung in the hand, representing an influence on activity in the physical world. He was stung in the throat when the ring was being manufactured. It is a picture of Ahrimanic forces penetrating into the organs of speech whereby the former magic creative power of the word is destroyed. In making the hammer the sting was between the eyes. For a moment Brock was blinded— Ahrimanic forces cause human beings to be blind to the spiritual world. The hammer is short. The ego force is less powerful than it might have been.*

*The judgement is that the gifts from Sindri and Brock have the greater value. It could not be otherwise since the approaching age is one where materialistic forces will predominate.*

*Spear and ring are presented to Odin. The gifts are appropriate since Odin is the creator of speech and the supreme leader. (The names Odin/Wotan are probably connected with the old English word 'brethen', to breathe.)*

*Frey received the magic ship and the boar. Frey is the one who influences the weather, growth and fertility, human desires.*

*Thor's wife gets the earthly hair and Thor the hammer. His task is to combat the giants. When roused the blood circulates quicker, the heart beats faster. In the blood is the ego force but the hammer is deficient. Even Thor succumbs on the day of Ragnarok.*

*A twisted mouth shows the ability to twist words.*

## Heimdall in Midgard

Odin knew that sometime there would be a last great battle with the giants and he wanted to have the right sort of people to help. He sent Heimdall to Midgard to arrange this. Heimdall disguised himself as Rig the Walker. Coming to a small cottage, he was made welcome by its inhabitants, a poorly dressed couple called Ai and Edda, Great-grandfather and Great-grandmother. He was given bread and broth, the best place to sit and at night, the warmest place to sleep—in a bed between the pair. He stayed for three days, then journeyed on.

After the moon had waxed and waned nine times, Edda bore a son. He was called Thrall, 'the serf'. Thrall grew quickly and he became a strong man with hard hands and thick fingers, broad back, big feet and a crude looking face. He married a wandering girl called Thir, 'the drudge', somewhat like himself. Their children worked on the land, labouring, building fences, tilling the ground, tending cattle and pigs, and doing all menial tasks.

Next Heirndall came to a house where a well-dressed couple lived, called Afi and Amma, Grandfather and Grandmother. He was made welcome, given a meal of boiled veal, bread, butter and beer, given the best place to sit and, at night, the warmest place to sleep—in between the pair. He stayed for three days, then journeyed on.

After the moon had waxed and waned nine times, Amma bore a son. He was called Karl, the Craftsman. He grew up to be a sturdy, good-looking, happy man. He was skilled at ploughing, in building houses, in making carts and wheels. He married the daughter of a freeman and their children became warriors, landowners and craftsmen.

In journeying further Heirndall came to a fine hall where a goodly couple lived dressed in fine clothes, with fine clean white hands. They were called Father and Mother. He was made welcome, given white bread, roast meat, cheese, vegetables and wine, all served in silver ware on a white tablecloth. He was given the best place to sit and, at night, the warmest place to sleep—in bed between the pair. He stayed for three days, then journeyed on.

After the moon had waxed and waned nine times, Mother bore a son. He was called Jarl, the Chieftain, and he grew up to be a handsome man, learning to ride, to shoot, to wield spear and shield.

Time went by and after many years Heimdall returned to Midgard. Thrall and Karl were good and useful men but Jarl was the most suitable for Odin's purpose. Heimdall made himself known to him, called him his son, and taught him the magic of the runes.

Jarl gathered brave men about him. He married the accomplished daughter of a wise and worthy man. Their children became rulers and understood many things hidden to others. One of their sons became a king.

He knew the language of the birds and from his father he learned all the things that Heimdall knew, - of the war-to-come between the Aesir and the giants and how Odin had decreed that all who fell fighting bravely in battle were to be brought to Asgard to help the army of the Aesir in the great battle on the last day.

*Heimdall is described as having had nine mothers and as possessing keen earthly senses. In an earthly incarnation it would mean that he possessed knowledge of the nine worlds and was a high initiate. It was his task to help educate humanity to clarity of thought and sense awareness to combat the old atavistic clairvoyance of Atlantis.*

*The children of Heimdall are known as the Holy Race. This picturesque story of Rig and his adventures is often interpreted as the story of the origin of the three classes of Viking society: the Thralls, servants and serfs; the Karls, craftsmen and farmers; the Jarls, hunters, fighters, aristocracy.*

*There is however a deeper meaning. It is not a story of physical generation but of stages of development and ennoblement The important element is that fresh forces are generated, new impulses are implanted in humanity and those that mature in the right way can be enhanced. Strong and mature souls are needed to combat evil.*

*Becoming king means becoming the one who knows. The king is the initiate who can direct and inspire.*

## The Deeds of Thor

Thor is a well-loved character in the Norse Stories and since we now appreciate what he represents, this is no cause for wonder. Hence he merits a section for himself.

He is continually doing battle with the giants and many are the tales of his prowess.

The story of the stealing of his hammer is a great favourite with children. In his teaching days the author was inspired to put this into verse and this original poem is included here. The combination of alliteration and rhyme may offend the purists but children will recite it with a rare gusto.

### Thor's Hammer is Stolen

One morning Thor's hammer was missing. He called on Loki to find out where it had gone. Loki discovered that it had been stolen by the giant, Thrym, and that the giant would only return it if Freya became his bride.

The Aesir were very worried at the news but Heimdall suggested that Thor should dress up as Freya and present himself. Loki went along as the serving maid.

At Thrym's court the giant was somewhat surprised at his bride's appetite and even more so by her fiery looks. Loki explained that she was pining for love and had neither been able to eat nor sleep.

The hammer was produced as the bride price but as soon as Thor had it in his hands, he despatched Thrym and all the rest of the giants present.

### Thor's Journey to Giantland

One morning the mighty Mjölnir was missing.
Wild, on waking, was Thunderer Thor.
He bristled his beard, his breast was bursting
And his face a fierce frown wore.

"Loki," said he, "My hammer is gone.
Without my weapon my works are weak.
Find thou Freya and dress in her feathers,
That which is stolen, I beseech thee to seek."

The feather dress whirred and Loki flew fleetly,
Leaving Thor the Thunderer to fume and fret.
To the realm of the Giants he rode and soon reached it.
There Thrym, on a mound, the master he met.

Thrym saw him and said, "I see thy deception.
What leads thee, Loki, alone to this land?"
And Loki told of the trouble in Asgard,
Thor's howl when the hammer was gone from his hand.

Thrym looked at Loki and loudly he laughed:
"Down deep in the depths of a dark mountainside
Thor's hammer is hidden. That hole is its home
Till beautiful Freya you bring for my bride."

Up Loki soared and to Asgard sped swiftly.
In a second Thor saw him and stood by his side.
"Thor, thy hammer is hidden, the Giant King keeps it,
Unless beautiful Freya we bring for his bride."

Quickly the gods all gathered together,
To talk of the tidings Loki had told.

And Freya grew fierce and scaldingly snorted:
"'I will not travel north, I will never be sold."

Thus spoke she, and suddenly silence descended.
No murmur nor mutter was made by the throng,
Till Heimdall, the hero, at last his voice lifted:
"Thor himself shall ride out and shall right us this wrong."

"The bridal veil let brave Thor bear,
And down to his knees let us drape a maid's dress.
On his breast precious stones and fine silver shall sparkle,
And a pretty pink cap on his head let us press."

Thor arose in a rage and wrathfully roared:
"Would you make me a maid, me, Thunderer Thor?"
But Loki was crafty and cunningly cried:
"Gainst the frost giants fearful, we can fight nevermore."

Thor gasped and gazed on the garden of Asgard.
"I must have my hammer to defend our home.
I bid you, my brothers, the bridal veil bind.
To the cold giant country let me quickly be gone."

Then forth Loki stood and now sweetly he spoke:
"As thy maidservant, Thor, go I thither with thee.
I will dress as a girl and together we'll go.
What a beautiful maid for the bride I shall be."

In the palace of Thrym a proud feast was prepared
To welcome the wanderers and wish them well.
For the maidens a dish of fine dainties was set,
But Thor ate an ox, his craving to quell.

Then he seized and he swallowed eight fat salmon,
And he drank to the bottom three barrels of beer.
Thrym waited and watched and in wonder he murmured:
"This maiden bites hard and heftily here."

Close by there sat the serving maid still,
And the words of the giant well answered she:
"From food has Freya eight nights fasted,
So lively her longing to look at thee."

Thryin crossed to kiss the beautiful bride,
For his heart was in haste, so hot his desire,
But on lifting the veil a length back he leapt:
"This maid gives a glance like a furnace on fire."

Close by there sat the serving maid still,
And the words of the giant well answered she:
"No sleep has Freya for eight nights found
So lively her longing to look at thee."

Then laughing and loud spoke the giant's leader:
"Bring here now the hammer to hallow the bride.
On the knees of the maiden lay Mjölnir, the mighty,
And myself then softly will sit by her side."

Thor seized his hammer and swung it swiftly
Above his body, around in a ring.
With a rushing of air and a roar of rage
He cracked the crown of the giant king.

He stood and swung it a second time
And down the giants dropped all dead.
A third time the Thunderer heaved his hammer.
A castle crumbled. Ruins stood there instead.

At last stood Loki and Thor alone;
And so his hammer saved Odin's son.

*If the ego is weak or asleep, evil forces can act. The story says 'one morning. Obviously Thor had been asleep when the giant stole his hammer. The ego forces had succumbed to a powerful retarding influence. This came from the realm of Jotunheim, the region we have already characterised as Ahrimanic. Ahriman's aim is to make man think that the physical world is the only real one. In this case he wants to gain possession of the regenerative forces, that is, to persuade men that sex is only a physical matter.*

*Although Loki-Lucifer's influence is often negative, it is here that his positive side is seen. Lucifer gives the human being initiative, enthu-*

*siasm, self-awareness. Loki restores Thor's confidence.. i.e. he strengthens the ego. The hammer is retrieved and the retarding powers destroyed.*

## Thor's Journey to Utgard

One day Thor decided to visit Utgard to settle a few scores with the giants. Loki went with him. Thor harnessed his two goats to his chariot and they set off. In the evening they came to a lonely farm. The farmer apologised for not having much food available. Thor slaughtered his two goats, skinned them and put the meat in the pot. When it was cooked, they made a meal of the flesh but Thor said that on no account should any of the bones be broken. They should be collected and placed on the skins. However, Thialfi, one of the farmer's children, split a thigh bone in order to suck out the marrow.

In the morning Thor and Loki got up, refreshed, and Thor waved his hammer over the bones and skins. Immediately the goats sprang up full of life, but one of them limped. Thor was furious but was finally appeased, saying he would take the farmer's two children with him as recompense, to be his servants. Their names were Thialfi and Rokva.

The travellers left the goats and went forward on foot. They reached the seashore, found a boat and crossed the sea. They met no-one and journeyed inland. Evening came and there seemed to be no shelter but then they came across a strange building like an enormous hall but open at one end. They entered and lay down to sleep but there was a noise and a rumbling like an earthquake. They crept further into the hall and found a little side room where they made themselves as comfortable as they could.

When it was light, they came out and found an enormous giant asleep on the ground. He woke up and addressed Thor. He said he was called Skrymir and he had come to guide the visitors to Utgard. He picked up their sleeping quarters, indeed they were his glove and the small place where they had slept was the opening for his thumb.

The giant offered to carry their bag of provisions and put it in his own. They journeyed on and bedded down for the night under a great oak tree. The giant went to sleep but Thor and Loki could not unfasten the strap of his knap-sack in order to get food and so they went hungry.

Thor was angry and realised the giant was playing tricks with them. He swung his hammer at what he thought was the giant's head but the giant only murmured something about a leaf falling on him. Thor tried again and the giant asked if an acorn had fallen on him. A third time Thor struck but all the giant did was to grumble about a bird dropping something on him.

In the morning they all got up. The giant pointed them towards the east and said that he himself must go off towards the north.

That night the travellers came to a stronghold, squeezed through the iron bars of the gates and came into the hall of the giant king, Utgardloki. The king said that only masters of some craft or special skill could stay there and asked what they could offer,

Loki said that he could eat faster than anyone else but when put to the test, he failed.

Thialfi challenged anyone to run as fast as himself but he also failed.

Thor said he would have a drinking match. He was given a horn which seemed rather large and had a long point, but try as he would, he could not empty it. The king taunted him and brought in his cat. He challenged Thor to lift it from the floor but the cat simply arched its back and kept its feet on the ground. Thor was cross and offered to wrestle with someone. The giant sent for Elli, his old foster mother, but Thor was powerless against her.

After these contests they feasted and slept.

The next day the visitors prepared to leave and the giant king was very gay and courteous. He accompanied them out of Utgard and asked if they had ever met giants more powerful than himself and his entourage. Thor admitted he had come off second best. Loki smiled secretly.

Then the giant confessed that he had used tricks. He explained that he himself was the giant Skrymir and the blows Thor gave would have killed him except for the fact that he rolled out of the way and he showed dents in the hills where the hammer had landed.

The contestant who beat Loki was fire. The runner who beat Thialfi was thought. The horn had its point connected to the sea and Thor's drinking had caused an ebb. The tides would now flow in memory of that feat.

The cat was really the Midgard serpent and Elli was Old Age. The giant advised Thor not to come again but by now Thor was seething with anger. He grasped his hammer and swung it round, only to find that Utgardloki was gone. In the distance the stronghold of Utgard had disappeared.

The travellers returned to the farmhouse where the goats and chariot had been left and made their way back to Asgard.

*Thor represents the power of the ego. In the human being it is the ego which is, or should be, the directing force. It should control the natural impulses within the soul and fight against evil forces without. This is why Thor is continually represented as fighting with the giants. Often there is a reference to his journeys to the east. Historically the Germanic tribes were continually at war with degenerate people living to the east and this bit of folk history has become incorporated in the story.*

*Utgard is the outer kingdom, It is the same as Jotunheim. The giants of Jotunheim have already been described as representing Ahrimanic forces. It is therefore not surprising that Loki goes along with Thor. It is the Loki-Luciferic influence which opens the way for Ahriman.*

*The first part of the story is a waking-sleeping experience. Goats are a symbol for curiosity. Curiosity means exercising the senses. When the human beings are awake, i.e. when the ego is within the bodily organism, they receive sense-impressions. When they are asleep the goat nature within is dead. It is nighttime on the farm; the goats are killed and their meat is digested during sleep, Similarly sense impressions are digested at night. In the morning the ego returns to receive sense impressions again; the goats are reconstituted. However, one bone has been damaged and one goat limps. If physical organs are not adequate, sense impressions are distorted.*

*The goats are left behind. It is now a matter of a contest with evil powers in a supersensible realm. The children are extensions of the self.*

*The travellers have certain adventures and meet Skrymir and it is obvious from the eventual outcome that they have been the victims of deceit, a typical Ahrimanic ploy. They are asked to demonstrate special powers but fail each time. It is a demonstration of the fact that the ego is not sufficiently developed. It has not sufficient power to deal with the opposing forces. Elli (Old Age) represents death but Thor cannot overcome her. The significance is that death is still the last enem,; the time has not yet come for conscious transition to the spiritual world.*

*The giant they meet is called Utgardloki, Loki of the outer kingdom, yet he is obviously not Loki. The power we know as Loki influences the inner world. The negative power in the other world, the Loki of the outer kingdom, is his counterpart, Ahriman. It may be that the writer of the story did not differentiate, between the two powers of evil. Neither did Goethe. The figure of Mephistopheles in his Faust is a mixture of both.*

## Thor Fetches Hymir's Cauldron

Not all giants were enemies of the Aesir. There was the sea-god, Aegir, who used to invite them on occasion to a party.

Once the Aesir arrived unexpectedly at his hall, having great thirst. Thor asked Aegir to provide mead to drink but the latter said that he would first have to brew it and that he had no cauldron big enough. He suggested that Thor should find one. Tyr said that his step-father, the giant Hymir, had one and that they should fetch that.

Accordingly Thor and Tyr set out for Hymir's dwelling which was on the edge of the world. At first they travelled in Thor's chariot drawn by his goats but left these with a friend and continued on foot.

They came to Hymir's hall where a monster met them in the form of a female with nine hundred heads. They entered, however, and were met by a most beautiful woman. She greeted Tyr as her son and told the visitors that Hymir did not welcome guests at first and that they should hide until his annoyance had subsided.

When Hymir came home she told him that he had guests who were sitting behind one of the pillars. He looked at the pillar and it shattered to pieces bringing down the beam on which several cauldrons hung. All broke to pieces except the biggest one. After a while he deigned to give them supper. Thor ate so much that Hymir said they would have to go hunting if they wanted more meals, but Thor preferred to go fishing. Thor and Hymir set out in a boat and Hymir caught two whales but Thor wanted to bait the Midgard Serpent. He hooked it and tried to draw it into the boat but Hymir became frightened and cut the line.

Reaching land, Thor hauled the boat, the whales and the oars to Hymir's hall. This caused anger in the giant as he had appeared to be the weaker and he declared he would only recognise as a strong man one who could smash a certain goblet. Thor took it and threw it against a stone pillar and the pillar was smashed to bits but the goblet remained whole. Hymir's wife whispered to Thor that he should throw it at Hymir's head. This he did and the goblet shattered. Hymir now said, "What is mine is now yours." Tyr tried to lift the cauldron but was not able to move it. Then Thor picked it up and they went on their way. Thor happened to look round and saw a host of giants coming after them so he put down the cauldron, seized his hammer and slew them all.

So they brought the cauldron to Aegir and he was able to brew the mead the gods required.

*The story of Hymir's cauldron tells us that the gods were short of drink. Hymir is obviously related to Ymir. He belongs to the past. The desire of the gods for mead signifies the wish to distil some of the old wisdom, to bring it up to date, so to speak. Clearly the one best fitted to find the means is Thor, supported by Tyr—ego forces supported by the will.*

*At first Thor and Tyr travel in a chariot pulled by Thor's goats. Then they proceed on foot, i.e. they leave the sense world. (Hymir lived on the edge of the world.) A monster met them, then a beautiful woman—spiritual experiences in the process of initiation. Hymir is not anxious to receive visitors. His eyes demonstrate supernatural forces but he finally offers supper to his guests. The old order does not change so easily.*

*He suggests they go hunting but Thor opts for fishing. Thor is related to the liquid element, the flowing blood. He tries to catch and destroy the Midgard Serpent but is frustrated by Hymir. The ego is in conflict with the wild passions but is hindered in subduing them. The fact is that Hymir is a Storm giant, working in the astral forces and therefore has a relationship with Loki's offspring, the Midgard Serpent. He is therefore not anxious to see the serpent destroyed.*

*Reaching land Thor hauls up the boat together with two whales which Hymir caught. The latter is jealous of his strength. He wants further tests. Hymir gives Thor a goblet to break by throwing it against a pillar. The goblet reminds one of the grail. It holds spiritual substance, albeit old in this case. The pillar breaks but not the goblet.*

*Harder than the pillar however is Hymir's head, representing old ossified forces. The goblet shatters on meeting it and Hymir recognises that his time has come. Without further ado he hands over the cauldron but it is difficult to carry and only Thor can manage. Old forces rally once more to prevent its being taken away but Thor overcomes them. The power of the ego is paramount.*

## Thor Fights the Giants Geirrodur and Rungnir

The giant Geirrodur lived in a great castle in Jotunheim.

Purposely Loki spoke one day in Asgard about this giant in the presence of Thor, saying how Geirrodur would like to meet Thor and praising the giant's hospitality. Thor was flattered and agreed to go with Loki on a visit. The latter persuaded him to leave his hammer behind lest taking it would appear unseemly behaviour.

On the way the travellers stayed for a night at the hall of Grid, a giantess who was friendly to the Aesir. When Loki was asleep, Grid told Thor the true nature of the giant which was very different from being hospitable. She offered to lend him her own belt of strength, iron gloves and unbreakable staff.

The next morning Thor and Loki continued on their journey and came to a great rushing bloody torrent. Thor, thanks to the loan of Grid's treasures, got across safely but Loki was swept back to the shore and took the opportunity to go back home to Asgard.

Thor came to Geirrodur's castle and was met by his troll servants. They took him to a guest room and motioned him to a chair where he sat down and fell asleep. Suddenly he awoke to find himself rising but he put the unbreakable staff against the roof and pushed himself down again. There was a horrible cry from under the chair. The two daughters of the giant had intended to squash Thor against the roof but he had turned the tables on them and now they lay dead.

The servants took Thor to the great hall where many fires were burning and where, at one end, the giant awaited him. Geirrodur had tongs in his hand and with them he picked up a red hot ball. He threw it at Thor. Thor was wearing the iron gloves and caught it. The giant dodged behind a pillar. Thor threw the ball back. It passed through the pillar, through the giant, through the wall, and buried itself in the earth outside.

With Grid's rod he set about all the trolls and smashed their skulls. Then he went off, returning the things he had borrowed to Grid and thinking about two-faced Loki.

Another giant with whom Thor had a contest was Rungnir, the Mountain giant, who had a skull of stone. Rungnir had challenged him to a duel and they arranged to meet where Asgard borders on Jotunheim.

Thor had his hammer and Rungnir was armed with a whetstone. They threw their weapons at the same time and hammer and whetstone met in mid-air. The stone was shattered and a piece stuck in Thor's head, causing him pain, but the hammer flew on unharmed and struck the giant dead.

The Aesir asked the witch Groa to sing charms over Thor's head and as she did so the pain left him. Then Thor gave her news of her husband which so excited her that she forgot the charms and ran away. The splinter stayed in Thor's head but he suffered no more pain.

*Geirrodur.*

*This is almost a classical encounter—ego forces versus the two adversaries, Lucifer and Ahriman. As usual Loki-Lucifer is the instigator of events.*

*Loki entices Thor, as a result of which Thor confronts Geirrodur. When Thor has fallen for Loki's blandishments, the latter retires.*

*On the way to meet the giant Thor is given help, i.e. there are helpful agencies available as well as hindering ones. Thor himself owns a girdle of strength, but here he is lent one, representing the forces of the cosmos. The iron gloves are connected with the iron of the blood and the unbreakable staff is the power of the ego.*

*The story shows how the ego powers meet difficulties, how they are helped, attacked, but are finally triumphant.*

*Rungnir.*

*Again the two forces meet. Thor's weapon however is the stronger—the ego force wins. But something of the old powers infect the new. They can be made harmless but final eradication is something that belongs to the future.*

## The Brising Necklace

Although her father was of the Vanir, Freya lived happily with her husband in Asgard.

It happened one day that she took a stroll through Midgard, followed by Loki although she did not know this. She came to the borders of Svartalfheim, where the black dwarfs live. They set a trap for her. In a wide cave they set up their forge and made the most wonderful necklace ever seen.

Freya came by and immediately wanted to buy it. The four dwarfs who had made it would accept no money but said that she could have it if she agreed to be wedded for a day and a night to each of them in turn. She was so dazzled that she forgot her husband, forgot her home and Asgard, and agreed.

She returned to Asgard with the necklace. Loki also returned and reported to Odin what had happened. Odin ordered him to get it.

Loki turned himself into a fly to get into Freya's bedroom when she was asleep. She was wearing the necklace but the clasp was under her head. Loki turned himself into a flea and bit her cheek. This caused her to turn her head and Loki, resuming his own form, undid the clasp, took the necklace and made his way out.

When Freya woke and found her door unbolted, she guessed what had happened and complained to Odin. He, however, declared that she could only have the necklace back if she agreed to stir up wars between men. Then there would be battles and slain men and she must use her charms to give new life to corpses. As soon as a warrrior was killed, he must be brought back to life to fight again. She must always wear the necklace as a reminder.

*Dark powers seek to hinder progress. The advent of Njord, of the Vanir, in Asgard, signified a change from human clairvoyant perception and innocent reproduction to thinking and conscious sexual generation, as already explained. These new aspects are represented by Frey and Freya.*

*Freya is now tempted to indulge in the past.*

*A golden necklace consists of a number of links and, when worn, it hangs in the proximity of the larynx. Gold is reminiscent of the golden age, the age of the Vanir; as one link of a chain is connected with the next so in the chain of time are the generations of human beings. At one time memory was something that passed through the generations. An individual had the ability to remember the deeds of his ancestors through the close blood relationship. In the age of the Vanir, the power of the word was creative.*

*In desiring the necklace, therefore, Freya is being tempted to look back. Soul forces revert to earlier conditions.*

*Loki, however, is observing. He is concerned with forward development, albeit in his own interest. Loki-Lucifer brought human beings into physical existence, gave them conscious sexuality, consciousness of self; he affected speech so that its original power was lost. Different languages developed. Hence Loki is concerned with regard to Freya's adventures and reports them to Allfather Odin.*

*Odin turns the situation to his advantage. Stirring up wars, dying in battle and being revivified have to do with the fact that those who die young have a reserve of unused forces which live on in the spiritual world and support new generations of the race. In a time of growing intellectuality, also ordained, life forces are required as a balance. Odin requires that his race (the Germanic peoples) receive rejuvenating forces.*

*The representative of sexual love is well qualified to do this. To wear the necklace as a reminder is to be constantly aware of forward evolution.*

## Odin visits Vafthrudnir

One day Odin decided to visit the giant Vafthrudnir to test his wisdom. He came into the giant's presence in the guise of Gagnrad which means 'one who is well advised'. He was made welcome and he asked if it were possible that the giant knew everything. Vafthrudnir was offended and said that his visitor would not leave alive unless he proved to be wiser than he himself. They made a wager and put their heads as stakes.

Vafthrudnir began the questioning. He put questions about the alternation of day and night, and of the world of gods and humans. Gagnrad answered them all correctly. Then it was his turn.

He asked the giant about the creation of the world, its evolution, its future and the day of Ragnarok. All these questions were answered correctly. Odin asked, "Who will be alive when the long winter ends?" and the giant answered, "Lif and Lifthrasir live hidden in Hoddmimir's grove. From them a new race will develop." Odin asked, "Who will guide after the Day of Ragnarok?" and the giant answered, "Vidar and Vali will guide after the Day of Ragnarok. Modi and Magni will wield Mjölnir" Odin asked, "How will the sun rise when Fenris has swallowed ii?" and the giant answered, "The sun will have a daughter not less beautiful than herself who will follow the mother's path." Odin asked, "What did Odin whisper in Balder's ear before he was burnt on the funeral pyre?"

The giant was startled. Looking closely at his visitor, he now recognised him and said, "Only Odin can know what he whispered in his son's ear. My time is over. I have pitted myself against Odin. He is wiser than I." Those were the last words he ever spoke.

*The story is concerned with the passing of old powers and the advent of new.*

*The conversation is a relic of an initiation process. Wagering the head means offering the whole self. The wise one tests the knowledge and suitability of the would-be initiate. Vafthrudnir was a friendly giant. He could instruct in past evolution and, to some extent, could know of things to come. But there was something new which was beyond his experience and knowledge. The return of Balder means the possibility of a new form of spiritual vision, but this is brought about because a new power (Christ) enters evolution. This the giant did not know.*

## The Gift of a Queen

Once a poor shepherd was in the mountains when he came across an opening into a glacier. Venturing inside he found himself in a room lined with jewels and in the commanding presence of a beautiful woman who held a small bunch of blue flowers in her hand. It was Frigga.

The shepherd was overawed and sank to his knees but Frigga bade him rise and asked what souvenir he would like to take back home with him. The shepherd asked for the flowers in her hand and was commended for his wisdom. He was given the flowers and some seed which would produce more of the same.

When he reached home his wife was cross because he had not chosen a jewel but he planted the seeds and in due course he had a lovely crop of starry blue flowers.

When they had withered and the seeds were ripe, Frigga, in the guise of an old woman, visited the pair and showed them how to spin the stalks into thread and to weave the thread into linen, for this plant was the flax.

Soon many people came to buy the wonderful material and the shepherd and his wife became prosperous.

*The story is an illustration of inspired wisdom. In times past people were in direct contact with the gods and received instruction from* them.

## The Death of Balder

Balder was usually happy and gay but he began to have bad dreams. A sadness came over him which troubled him and the Aesir as well. They asked him the cause but he could only say that he had forebodings of death.

Odin was determined to find out more. He saddled his horse and rode down to the kingdom of Hela. Instead of entering her hall which was richly decorated as if an important visitor were expected, he turned aside to the grave of the Volva, the seeress. With chants and spells he called her forth and asked for whom Hela's hall was so richly adorned. She told him that Balder was expected, that he would be killed by Hoder and that Vali (another son of Odin's) would avenge him. She also told him that Loki would be chained but that he would break loose. She foretold of a great winter on earth and then was silent.

On his return Frigga told him that he had no need to worry because she had exacted a promise from all things that they would not harm Balder. The Aesir decided to put it to the test. They threw pebbles, spears and axes at Balder but none would touch him and there was great merriment.

Loki watched with distaste and, turning himself into an old woman, he sought out Frigga. Pretending to be mystified at the gay proceedings he found out that Frigga had missed one plant which she had considered of no importance, namely, the mistletoe.

Changing back to his own form after leaving Frigga, Loki sought and found some mistletoe. He made a dart from its twigs and came back to the party. He sympathised with blind Hoder at not being able to join in the fun, then put the dart in his hand and guided it as Hoder threw it.

The dart struck Balder and he fell dead, to become a ghost in Hela's kingdom. There was consternation among the Aesir and a feeling of horror. Loki slunk away.

Frigga asked if anyone would ride to the lower realm to offer a ransom for Balder's return. Hermod, the swiftest of the Aesir, volunteered. Odin lent him his horse, Sleipnir, and gave him his ring to give to Balder.

Hermod rode for nine nights. He crossed a bridge which no man alive had crossed before. He came to Hela's hall and there sat, in the seat of honour, the spirit of Balder. He heard Hela pronouncing judgements on the dead. He spoke to her and asked if Balder might be allowed to return to Asgard. Her answer was that, if all things dead or alive should weep for Balder, then he might return but if a single one fail, he must stay with her. Balder would not accept Odin's ring and sent it back. Hermod rode away.

He returned to Asgard and brought Hela's message. Immediately the Aesir sent messengers all over the world and it seemed as if all things, all people, and even giants and elves would weep for Balder. However, one giantess, Thokk, sitting in a deep cave in Jotunheim, refused. The Aesir had no doubt that this giantess was either Loki himself or one of his minions.

The Aesir built a huge funeral pyre on Balder's ship but the ship was so heavy that they could not launch it and had to call on the services of the giantess, Hyrrokin, whom they summoned from Jotunheim. When the ship was in the water, they took Balder's body to it and placed it on the funeral pyre. Nanna's heart broke and she died. Her body was placed by the side of Balder's. Odin placed his ring on Balder's finger and whispered in his ear. A vast concourse assembled: Aesir, dwarfs, elves and giants. A torch was put to the funeral pyre, the ship released and slowly it sailed out to sea. The flames shone brightly and rose into the air until it seemed that the ship touched the horizon when suddenly it was gone.

*Balder was known as the Beautiful. He had an aura of light around him. In his presence was joy, happiness and healing forces. No-one disputed with him. He quarrelled with no-one. His death is a prelude to the twilight of the gods when men would finally lose all perception of the spiritual world. When Balder has nightmares and forebodings of death, it signifies a premonition of changed times.*

*Balder represents the clairvoyant consciousness which was aware of the spiritual in nature; his wife, Nanna, the innocent forces of the plant world. The Norse peoples were aware of divine beings around them, manifesting in colour, speech, plants, animals and men. They felt too that divine beings were active in the elements, in fire, water, air and earth but they also felt that a time of darkness was coming. It was a prelude to the modern age when spiritual vision has disappeared, when nature has become soul-less, when only sense perception is considered to yield the truth and things are judged from the material standpoint of weight and measure. Thought takes the place of vision; hence the reference to the time of winter. Earth existence becomes wintry because thought is cold.*

*Odin knew that times would change but it was confirmed through his visit to the seeress. He visits her, calling himself Wegtam. This means 'one who knows the way'. The phrase means an initiate. He travels on the magic horse Sleipnir signifying a journey in spirit. The seeress points to the binding of Loki and the time when he will be freed as well as of the death of Balder and subsequent events. She speaks about the winter earth condition. At a certain point she refuses to speak further. She was announcing that this way of initiation is now closed.*

*Lucifer was responsible for the Fall, i.e. the descent of the human being into the physical world. In the form of Loki he continues his efforts. He uses the mistletoe to make a weapon.*

*The mistletoe is a peculiar plant, It has emancipated itself from the sun rhythm, It fruits at the winter solstice. It does not belong to the earth properly. It has no root. It is a parasite. It is of an order different from other earthly creations and hence Loki can make use of it. Hoder represents the consciousness which is blind to the spiritual. He is an Ahrimanic force; so again Loki works with his counterpart to the apparent detriment of humanity. Balder dies and spiritual vision disappears. Spiritual light is no longer manifest and must be sought in another world. Hermod volunteers to seek it.*

*He travels nine nights, i.e. through the nine spheres. It is another picture of an initiation process. Odin has sent his ring to Balder. He wants Balder to retain memories of the upper world but Balder returns it, i.e. the memory of the spirit shall remain on earth. Neither is Balder released. We are being told that at this stage in evolution spiritual vision is lost. Only if all things weep tears for Balder can he be released. The giantess refuses. She portrays the hardened human soul which has dried up through lack of spiritual insight, so spiritual insight is no more.*

*Balder's ship sails away. The funeral pyre burns brightly. The light returns to the light. The spirit is quickly dispersed into the spheres of air.*

*The message that Odin gives to Balder is that he will return, i.e. what sinks into the depths of the human soul is not lost forever. A metamorphosis takes place. For the present spiritual vision is lost and earthly consciousness, for the sake of human freedom, must be developed. Eventually there will be a renewal. Physical and spiritual science will unite. Balder and Hoder will be allies. Their sons will reach the 'Far Home of the Winds', i.e. the spiritual world.*

*Why were Odin's words in Balder's ear considered secret? The reason is that new forces of cognition will develop which cannot be deduced from past evolution. It is a foreshadowing of the Christ.*

## Frey Falls in Love with a Giant's Daughter

One day Frey sat in Odin's high seat and looked out over all the worlds. He looked towards Jotunheim and saw the hall of the giant Gymir. Coming out of the hall was his daughter, Gerda. She raised her arms and it seemed as if the whole sky and earth grew brighter. It was like a flash of icy bright light.

Frey fell madly in love with her. His heart ached. He was afflicted with melancholy. He could not eat. He could not sleep. Njord, his father, became very concerned about him. He called for Skirnir, Frey's servant, and asked him to find out about the trouble.

At first Frey would say nothing but after persuasion, he unburdened himself. Skirnir offered to fetch Gerda if he could have Frey's horse and magic sword. Frey agreed but he lived to regret it for his sword would have been useful on the day of Ragnarok.

Skirnir set off on the journey. He rode all night, over plains, over high mountains. He rode through a curtain of fire to reach Gymir's hall.

Gerda received him coldly. He offered gifts, eleven golden apples, even Odin's ring which he had acquired, but to no avail. Then he threatened her with the sword and the promise of bringing terrible curses down upon her if she did not agree to become Frey's bride.

At last she agreed but said that she would only come to Asgard after nine nights. Skirnir took the message back to Frey who showed great anguish at having to wait so long.

*At its simplest the story portrays a stage in human development which could be that of the single individual or humanity in general. Taking the case of the individual we observe that in the growth of a child a soul-spiritual being incarnates into a physical. One can observe the stages. This particular story represents the age of puberty. It is the age of physical maturity but at the same time it is the age when individual perception and independent judgement develop. The picture we are given is that of the appreciation of the sense world, which is overwhelming. The adolescent is not sure of himself. The sense world is full of attractions; it is also full of pitfalls unless entered with reason.*

*The story could also be looked upon as a nature myth since Frey is the god of fertility and Gerda represents the earth but there is also a larger view.*

*Skirnir means the 'shining one'. He represents Frey's alter ego. The name Gymir has some affinity with Ymir and thus signifies a material connection.*

*The events obviously take place after Balder's demise. The light of the spirit has gone out and the material world beckons.*

*Frey is the son of Njord, one of the Vanir. The age of the Vanir was one when men possessed primeval clairvoyance and when reproduction was unconscious. Njord married Skadi, a giantess, and their children are of mixed descent. The significance is that original clairvoyance and innocent reproduction have been superseded. Now there is thought and the power of imagination, and conscious sexual reproduction. Thought and imagination are symbolised in Frey's horse and sword. Frey now seeks to unite with the Jutun powers.*

*The Jotun forces, unless transformed, are destructive. This is the picture which Skirnir paints when he threatens and curses Gerda. The lower nature can run wild unless united with the higher. At the same time, forces of reason, which are cold and intellectual, need to be combined with those of heart and will.*

## Vali, the Avenger

Balder was dead. Hoder, even though he had cast the fatal dart in innocence, must die. Odin knew that his avenger must be the son of a mortal mother whom he must woo and who would survive Ragnarok. But he did not know who was to be his mortal wife and so sent Hermod on the horse Sleipnir to the wizard Rossthiof who lived in the utmost north. The wizard tried to entrap Hermod with his magic arts but Sleipnir was a wonderful horse and Hermod had with him Odin's runic staff with which he fended off evil beings.

Rossthiof came against him in the form of a giant, holding a rope with which he hoped to bind the horse and rider. But Hermod struck him with Odin's staff and then bound him with his own rope. At that, he was willing to answer the question as to who would be the mother of Balder's avenger.

He murmured spells and incantations and a vision rose before Hermod of a beautiful woman with a child in her arms. The child suddenly grew to be a youth. He had a bow and quiver. He drew an arrow and shot it. The vision faded.

Rossthiof explained that the woman was Rinda, the daughter of Billing, that the child was Vali, destined to be the avenger, and that Odin was to be the father but he would have to woo and win Rinda as a mortal man.

Hermod brought the message back to Odin who laid aside his -divine majesty. With his broad brimmed hat, his blue cloak and his spear, he went to Midgard. There he offered his services as an experienced warrior to King Billing.

An enemy was about to invade King Billing's lands and the disguised Odin undertook to lead the king's armies, saying that when he had proved his worth, he would try his luck with the beautiful Rinda.

He was victorious in the field but Rinda spurned him.

Not to be defeated, Odin left the court and returned in another disguise, namely, that of a goldsmith. His craftmanship was superb and he made a present for Rinda, thinking in this way to win her love. She rejected him.

He came again as a young and handsome warrior. This time Rinda seemed interested and agreed to meet him secretly but it was a trap and soldiers came to arrest him. Odin managed to escape but not before he had managed to touch Rinda with his magic stick.

After that she appeared to be mad. One day an old woman offered to cure her, stipulating that she must be alone and undisturbed with the girl for a time. This was agreed and the old woman was taken to Rinda's room and left there.

The old woman threw off her disguise and there stood Odin.

He spoke gently. She understood and consented to be his wife.

After a while Odin returned to Asgard. One day a child appeared asking for Odin, his father. As the Aesir watched, he grew from a child to a youth, from a youth to a man. He fitted an arrow to his bow and shot at Hoder who sank to the ground and died.

Hoder went down to the hall of Hela and there Balder greeted him with open arms and a smile on his face. There they passed the time pleasantly together until the Day of Ragnarok.

*When Odin consults the seeress, he is told that Vali will avenge Balder. She indicates that a hero-child will be born with new powers. It is in the world order that ancient clairvoyance shall disappear and humanity shall be blind to the spiritual world, i.e. Balder is killed by Hoder but it is also in the world order that spiritual blindness shall be overcome by the development of new forces at a stage higher than before, i.e, the advent of Vali. Vali represents these new forces which must be attained through effort as against those which were originally given by the gods. The path of development lies through the physical world, so Odin must marry a mortal woman.*

*Not any woman, however, is suitable, so Hermod, the messenger, seeks higher guidance. He travels on Sleipnir so it is obviously a spiritual journey. The episode is reminiscent of the time when man and woman were brought together on the instructions of an initiate, for a special soul to incarnate.*

*Odin's wooing reminds one of the prince in the fairy stories who has to overcome all manner of difficulties in order to win his princess.*

*His child comes to Asgard and grows suddenly into a man, i.e. in manhood he retains his childlike forces. He has not been contaminated. It is the same as the Biblical "unless ye become as little children, ye shall not enter the kingdom of heaven."*

*Vali shoots Hoder, signifying that blindness to the spiritual world will be overcome.*

*Vafthrudnir prophesied that Vidar and Vali would administer holy things after Ragnarok when Surtur's flames would have died out.*

## Loki's Insults

The Aesir had gone to a feast with Aegir, the god of the sea. Loki was there too but the pleasure and goodwill in the place made him cross. He was particularly annoyed when the servants were continually praised for their care and, picking up a knife, he stabbed one of them and ran away.

A little while later he came back. He was stopped at the entrance but pushed his way in, saying that he had every right to be there and claiming immunity from attack. As he came in, there was silence. He asked the reason and requested some refreshment. Bragi told him that he was unwelcome and received insults as a result.

Loki turned to Odin, reminding him of their age-old alliance whereupon Odin directed Vidar to give him a drink. Loki then began to insult each and every member of the Aesir present, reciting their misbehaviour and misdeeds. Only Vidar was spared. He then boasted about his achievements, one of which was to bring about the death of Balder.

At that moment Thor came home from a journey in the east. Loki insulted him too but Thor picked up his hammer and Loki made off as fast as he could, shouting that everything there would soon go up in flames.

*Loki reveals his nature in the episode with the servant. It would seem natural for the Aesir to retaliate when he returns but they were in a place of sanctuary and although Loki had broken faith, the others could not follow suit. There was silence because the Aesir knew that Loki would bring fresh trouble. Bragi, the spokesman of the gods, tried to avert it but to no avail.*

*The role of negative forces in evolution has already been described. Lucifer has a place in the world order. He cannot therefore be denied his place at the feast.*

*In creating the human being the gods had a goal but it was an ideal and ideals are not always realised, or at least only realised by devious ways. The gods were deflected by negative forces represented by Loki and now he taunts them with his successes. His insults are really a description of the influence he has had in the circle of the Aesir. Vidar is the only one who did not fall prey to the Luciferic forces. That is why he has a role after the day of Ragnarok.*

*Loki cannot confront the awakened ego forces and therefore runs when Thor appears.*

## Loki's Punishment

After the death of Balder and after Loki had made all his insulting remarks, the Aesir decided that he must be punished, Loki knew what to expect. He was frightened and ran away. He hid in a hut in a deserted part of Midgard near a river and busied himself making a net from linen twine. This was a craft which Loki invented.

Odin, however, from his high seat, saw him and the Aesir set out to catch him. Loki saw them approaching, quickly threw his net on the fire and jumped into the river, turning himself into a salmon.

The Aesir discovered the ashes of the net and made one themselves. They dragged the river with it. As Loki tried to jump over it, Thor caught him. Loki tried to wriggle out of Thor's grasp but in vain. He returned to his own shape.

The captive was taken to a deep cave and bound to three rocks with gut which turned to iron. One strand was round his neck; the other, his loins and the third, under the knee joints. They caused pain. Skadi hung a venomous serpent over his head so that poison would drip onto his face. Sigyn, his true wife, stayed by his side and held a bowl to catch the drops but when she had to turn away to empty it, the venom fell on his face and he writhed in pain. Every time that happened the earth quaked.

Loki lay there and there he stayed until the day of Ragnarok.

*The story is one of the suffering of humanity brought about by the influence of Lucifer.*

*Lucifer brought human beings to the physical world and Luciferic forces are at work in them. What are the consequences? Human beings transgress and try to escape the result of their own deeds. They are caught in their own net. The ego forces prevail but suffering is involved.*

*The picture of Loki as a salmon is very apt. He is a 'slippery customer'. Thor, wading in the water, seizes him.*

*Loki was tied to a rock in a cave with bands which turned to iron. This is a very strong indication of the physical world. Where he is tied, in the neck, loins and round the legs, he feels pain. These are parts of the body where the Lucifer influence has been strong—speech, reproduction and will impulses. Skadi, a member of the Jotuns, suspends a venomous snake over Loki's head. The poison of materialism drips onto him. When this happens, the earth quakes.*

*In the picture of Loki's suffering is reflected what men and women experience through his influence.*

## The Day of Ragnarok

Odin and the Aesir were aware that one day the whole world would perish. The giants in Jotunheim muttered threateningly. There was a shadow over Asgard. In Midgard men did evil which Loki had taught them. Odin himself did not know the future but looking towards Midgard he recognised a wise seeress, more far-seeing than any other. In his disguise with slouched hat and blue cloak he came to question her but she recognised him immediately. She told him of things past but he wanted to know of the future.

With their combined spells her spirit looked to the future and prophesied:

There will be a fearful winter which lasts for three years, throttling Midgard. Men will fight one another; brother will fight brother; sons will fight fathers; daughters will abuse their mothers. The faithful will be considered fools and the honest, liars. The wolves will catch the sun and moon. The stars will disappear. There will be earthquakes and all bonds will burst. Loki and Fenris will run free. The sea will rage and the Midgard serpent will creep onto the land. With the waters rising, the ship Naglfar —the ship made from dead men's nails—will break loose. It will be full of giants ready to attack and Loki will lead them.

The world tree will tremble. Dwarfs and elves will hold their breath. Heimdall will blow his horn. The Aesir gather for battle together with the warriors from Valhalla. As they ride over the rainbow bridge, it crashes. Thor attacks the Midgard serpent and kills it but himself dies from the serpent's venom. Loki and Heimdall cause one another's death. The Fenris Wolf devours Odin but is slain by Vidar. Vidar has magic shoes made from the bits and pieces of leather cut off from heels and toes when shoes are made. He puts one foot on Fenris's bottom jaw, takes hold of the upper and tears the wolf apart. The hell-hound Gram fights with Tyr and they kill one another. Surtur slays Frey and spreads fire all over the earth which sinks into the sea.

A new earth will arise, green, beautiful and fertile. Before it is eaten by the wolf the sun will give birth to a daughter who will shine and follow the same path in the sky. Vidar and Vali will survive, so will the two sons of Thor, Modi and Magni. They will be carrying Mjölnir. Back from Hela's kingdom will come Balder and Hoder as allies. Honir joins them.

Midgard will arise again from the waters, peopled by the descendants of a couple who survive by hiding in Hoddmimir's grove in the depths of Yggdrasil. Their names are Lif and Lifthrasir (Life and Life- supporter). A new Asgard will arise and there the blessed of men and women mingle with the Aesir. There will be a new earth. A great one will come, one whose name cannot be mentioned but whose power will embrace the earth. He is 'the Strong One from Above'.

Thus Odin learned of things to come and now we know what he whispered into Balder's ear: "you will return."

*Ragnarok is the equivalent of Twilight of the Gods. The stories tell of the Day of Ragnarok but twilight is a more apt expression since events stretch over a period of time. In fact the twilight begins when Odin offers his eye or even with the advent of Loki but the darkness is final when the world goes up in flames. The events between illustrate stages.*

*Although we speak of the twilight of the gods, it is not their light which goes out. The gods do not die. The twilight refers to the growing inability of human beings to perceive them. It lasts as long as they are blind to the spiritual world. When they achieve the new perception, the gods return.*

*At one time the Norse peoples had a natural clairvoyance. They perceived and experienced beings and happenings in the spiritual world. For them there lived in nature and in the cosmos higher beings with whose existence their own was intimately woven. Negative forces intervened. The direction of the mind was turned towards the physical world. Spiritual vision faded and eventually even the belief in things spiritual was lost. This was due to what we have characterised as the Ahrimanic influence. It leads eventually to the 'scientific' concepts of humanity, earth and the universe. The earth becomes a minor planet revolving round the sun with many others. The spiritual agencies of the universe are supplanted by mathematical concepts. Colours become vibrations; the human being evolves accidentally from some protoplasm on the seashore.*

*The loss of spiritual insight was felt as a catastrophe yet it was inevitable and an essential step in the progress of humanity. In losing contact with the spiritual world the human being was thrown back on him- or herself; the individual experienced freedom and independence and became ego conscious. This was the aim of the creator gods.*

*In becoming free, however, from divine guidance, individuals also became subject to forces of negation or retardation, designated Luciferic and Ahrimanic as already explained. So long as they hold these forces in balance and rule them, they are safe. When such forces get out of hand, destruction and catastrophe follow. This is what happens on the Day of Ragnarok.*

*Looking at world events today one could assume that historically the Day of Ragnarok is upon us. The human being is being attacked from all sides—drugs, rampant materialism, mass suggestion, wars and rumours of wars, the atom bomb.*

*The Bible tells the same story: "Nation shall rise against nation and kingdom against kingdom, and there shall be earthquakes in divers places; and there shall be famines and troubles." (Mark 13: 8) "The sun shall be darkened, and the moon shall not give her light, and the stars of heaven shall fall, and the powers that are in heaven shall be shaken. (Mark 13:24-25) From St. John's Revelation: "The sun became black as sackcloth of hair, and the moon became as blood, and stars of heaven fell unto the earth." (Rev. 6:12) But in Revelation 21:1, there is a little light: "And I saw a new heaven and a new earth, for the first heaven and the first earth were passed away."*

*A three year long winter is predicted. The three, in this case, is like the fairy tale hundred years. It means a period of time, a time of gathering darkness. Winter brings with it the absence of warmth and the significance is that the cold rational forces of the intellect prevail. As a result the earth and its inhabitants are in turmoil. Evil forces run riot.*

*The ship, Naglfar, lands, loaded with giants. The ship is made from the finger- and toenails of dead men, i.e. hard parts of the human body. The symbolism points to the Ahrimanic forces. Loki guides them. As usual, the Luciferic influence opens up the way for the Ahrimanic.*

*The world tree trembles. The tree is the symbol of the 'I am'. The ego is attacked. The tree has been damaged continually by Nidhogg and others but the attack is now intensified. The divine watchman blows his horn. Odin's selected warriors engage in battle. The rainbow bridge collapses, i.e. gods, humans, elementals, giants are all concerned. There is mutual destruction.*

*Odin has served his time. He is devoured by the Fenris Wolf but Vidar slays Fenris. Vidar's magic shoes are made of discarded bits of leather when people have their shoes cut to shape. Shoes are symbolic of treading the path of destiny. When bits are used for making shoes for gods, it signifies that gods take part in human destiny.*

*Surtur is the being who has gained control of the original fire of the divine creation, out of which the world was formed long before the Ymir age. His flaming sword sets the world on fire. Yggdrasil is consumed. The old world ends. The Odin race of human beings, with their natural clairvoyance and relationship* to the gods, dies. But death does not mean final destruction. *Death signifies a new beginning.*

*A new sun will shine in the heavens. It represents a new spiritual force. An event takes place in world history which re-establishes the possibility of progress in human evolution. A force has come into the world through which a new insight into the spiritual world may be gained. Vidar represents it. It is the force that was there in the beginning and now appears in manifestation. Vidar was never entangled in the events of the Fall. Through the Vidar forces the view is opened again to the spirit world. With the new clairvoyance comes the equivalent of the return of the gods. Vali is Odin's son by Rinda, the earth goddess; he also survives, i.e. a divine seed was planted in the earth which can now grow. A new race of gods will now inspire mankind—Thor's sons, Modi and Magni, symbolising the free individuality. Balder and Hodur return, i.e. spiritual vision will now be combined with earthly knowledge. Honir, who was away in a higher region, comes again.*

*Vafthrudnir told Odin that two would survive Ragnarok and would found a new race. They would be nourished by the morning dew. The spirit of the human being lives on. It unites with the life forces which were not destroyed. The new race can walk and talk with the gods. Heaven and hell are now re-constituted in the new consciousness. These things will be possible through the power of the Christ.*

*The inference is of the Second Coming. With the Advent of Christ the earth was, so to speak, revitalised, giving humanity the possibility of acquiring new powers of spiritual perception, but the effect is not immediate. The Day of Ragnarok, our present world crisis, will pass. Christ will not appear again in the flesh but peoples' minds will be attuned to the spiritual and Christ will be experienced in a supersensible realm. It will be the dawn of a new era.*

# Glossary

The names in the Norse stories have a significance in themselves. Unfortunately not all can be explained. An approximate translation is given here (in brackets) where possible.

| | |
|---|---|
| Aegir | The god of the sea. |
| Aesir | (Gods). The race of gods particularly close to the Norse peoples. |
| Allfather | One of Odin's names. |
| Angurboda | (Bringer of Evil). The giantess whom Loki married and who became the mother of , the three monsters: Fenris Wolf, Jormungand and Hela. |
| Asgard | (The Realm of the Aesir). |
| Audumla | (Cow without Horns, i.e. lacking hardening forces). She appeared out of the ice in Ginnungengap and Ymir drank from her milk. |
| Balder | Son of Odin, noted for his beauty and sweet nature. He was killed unwittingly by his blind brother, Hoder. |
| Baugi | Brother of Suttung the Giant. Odin used him to obtain the Mead of Poetry. |
| Bergelmir | The giant who escaped when Ymir and his companions were killed. |
| Bilskirne | (Clearing Weather). Thor's hall in Asgard. |
| Bragi. | Son of Odin and the giantess Gunnlod. Musician and poet. Husband of Iduna. |
| Breidablick | (Broad Outlook). Balder's hall in Asgard. |
| Brising | The name of a race of dwarfs. |
| Brock | The name of the dwarf who, with his brother Sindri, and at Loki's request, made gifts for the gods: Gullinbursti, Draupnir and Mjölnir. |
| Burl | Grandfather of Odin, Vili and Ve. |

| | |
|---|---|
| Draupnir | (Dripper). Odin's golden ring from which 'dripped' duplicates. |
| Elli | (The Old One). Utgardloki's foster mother. Odin wrestled with her and lost. |
| Fenris Wolf | (Fen = Marsh). A monster offsping of Loki and Angurboda. |
| Fjalar and Galar | Dwarfs who killed Kvasir and made the Mead of Poetry from his blood. |
| Forseti | (The Just One). Son of Balder and his wife, Nanna. |
| Frey and Freya | Son and daughter of Njord and Skadi. |
| Frigga | (Frau). Wife of Odin. Foremost among the goddesses. |
| Gagnrad | (A Well-Advised One). One of Odin's names. |
| Garm | The Nordic Cerberus. The hell-hound. |
| Geirrodur | One of the giants who was overcome by Thor. |
| Gerda | (From Earth). A frost giantess with whom Frey fell in love and eventually married. |
| Ginnungengap | (Enchanted Gulf). The original void between Niflheim andMuspelheim. |
| Gladsheim | (Home of Joy). The sanctuary of the Aesir. |
| Grid | A giantess friendly to the Aesir. She helped Thor in his struggle with Geirrodur. |
| Gullinbursti | (Golden-bristled). The boar made by the dwarfs, Brock and Sindri, and given to Frey. |
| Gullveig | (Gull = gold). The messenger from the Vanir to the Aesir who tried to burn her up. |
| Gungnir | (Gung = going). Odin's magic spear made by the dwarfs known as Ivaldi's sons. |
| Gunnlod | Daughter of the giant Suttung and guardian of the Mead of Poetry. Seduced by Odin to obtain the mead. |
| Gymir | (Descended from Ymir). Earthly one. |
| Heimdall | (The Bright One in the World-All). Guardian of the Rainbow bridge. |

| | |
|---|---|
| Hela | (Hell). Ruler of the underworld. Monster offspring of Loki and Angurboda. |
| Hermod | (The Courageous One). Messenger of the Aesir. |
| Himinbjorg | (The Castle of Heaven). The hall of Heimdall. |
| Hoder | The blind son of Odin who unwittingly killed his brother Balder. |
| Hvergelmir | (Whirling in the Helm = brain). The spring flowing from Niflheim. |
| Hoddmimir | (Mimir's Grove). A place of sanctuary underneath the World Tree. |
| Honir | The god who gave man the faculty of imagination. |
| Hymir | (Related to Ymir). Earthly. |
| Iduna | Keeper of the golden apples. Wife of Bragi, the musician. |
| Ivaldi | Dwarf whose sons made gifts for the gods. Father of Iduna. |
| Jarl | (Earl). |
| Jotunheim | Home of the Jotun giants. |
| Jormungand | The Midgard serpent. Monster offspring of Loki and Angurboda. |
| Kvasir | A wise man created from the spittle of the gods. The Mead of Poetry was made from his blood. |
| Lif and Lifthrasir | (Life and Life-supporter). Survivors of Ragnarok to re-people the earth. |
| Loddfafnir | (Drag on-slayer). |
| Loki | (Light, Lie). The Nordic Lucifer. |
| Lodur | (Blaze Up). The god who gave man circulation of the blood. |
| Magni and Modi | (The Strong and The Courageous). Sons of Thor who will wield the hammer in the new age, |
| Midgard | (The Middle Realm). The world of men and women. |

| | |
|---|---|
| Mimir | (Memory). The guardian of the well of wisdom. |
| Mjölnir | (The Crusher). The name of Thor's hammer. |
| Mundilfari | The father of the children who drove the chariots of the sun and moon. |
| Muspelheim | (Home of Fire). The warmth area in the creation story. |
| Naglfar | (Conveyance built from Human Nails). The ship bringing the giants to attack Midgard. |
| Nanna | (The Active One). Wife of Balder. |
| Nidhogg | (Envy). The dragon that gnaws at the roots of Yggdrasil. |
| Niflheim | (Home of Mist). The cold area in the creation story. |
| Njord | One of the Vanir who came to live in Asgard. Father of Frey and Freya. |
| Norns | The goddesses of Destiny. The Fates. |
| Odin | (The Breather?). Foremost of the gods. Master of the power of speech. |
| Ragnarok | (Fading of the Gods). The destruction of the old world. |
| Ratatosk | (Swift Teeth). The squirrel who runs up and down Yggdrasil sowing enmity between the eagle and Nidhogg. |
| Rig | (King). The name used by Heimdall when journeying on earth. |
| Rinda | The name of Odin's human bride. Mother of Vali. |
| Rokva | The farmer's daughter who became Thor's servant on his way to visit Utgardloki. |
| Rossthiof | The wizard who announced Odin's human bride. |
| Sindri | See Brock. |
| Sif | Thor's wife whose hair was cut off by Loki. |
| Sigyn | Loki's faithful wife. |

| | |
|---|---|
| Skadi | The giantess who married Njord. |
| Skidbladnir | (Formed from Leaf-thin Blades). A collapsible ship made by the dwarfs—sons of Ivaldi—and given to Frey. |
| Skirnir | (The Shining One). Frey's messenger sent to woo Gerda on his behalf. |
| Skrymir | (The Shocker) Utgardloki in the disguise of a huge giant. |
| Skuld | (What Should Be). The Norn who sees the future. |
| Sleipnir | (The Slipper—in the sense of to slip, slide). Odin's eight legged horse. Offspring of Loki and the giant's stallion. |
| Surtur | (Black). The evil one who waits in Muspelheim to set the world on fire. |
| Suttung | Giant who hid the Mead of Poetry in a mountain and set his daughter Gunnlod to guard it. |
| Svartalfheim | (Home of the Black Dwarfs). |
| Thialfi | Farmer's son who becomes Thor's servant on his visit to Utgardloki. |
| Thiassi | The giant who stole Iduna and her apples and was killed by the Aesir. |
| Thor | (Thunder). Odin's son. Guardian of gods and human beings. |
| Thrudwang | (Meadow of the Brave). Thor's estate in Asgard. |
| Thrym | King of the Frost giants. He stole Thor's hammer and paid with his life. |
| Tyr | Bravest of the Aesir. He sacrificed his hand that Fenris could be restrained. |
| Ull | Son of Odin, associated with archery and skiing. |
| Urd | (Primeval). The Norn who sees the past. |
| Utgardloki | (Loki of the Outer World). The giant who challenged Thor and won. |

| | |
|---|---|
| Vafthrudnir | (Master of Riddles). Giant who was challenged by Odin to a test of knowledge. |
| Vali | Son of Odin and a human mother. He survives Ragnarok. |
| Valhalla | (Hall of the Chosen Slain). Odin's hall where the dead warriors celebrate and await the Day of Ragnarok. |
| Valkyrs | (Warrior Choosers). Battle maidens who bring slain warriors to Valhalla. |
| Vanaheim | (Home of the Vanir). |
| Vanir | A race of gods older than the Aesir. |
| Verdandi | (Becoming, Coming into Existence). The Norn who sees the present. |
| Vidar | (Ruler, Master). Son of Odin who destroys the Fenris Wolf and survives Ragnarok. |
| Vili and Ve | Brothers of Odin. Vili gives man movement (Will?); Ve, sense organs. |
| Yggdrasil | (Ego-bearer). The World Tree. |
| Ymir | (Primeval Human Being). The giant from whom the world and human form were fashioned. |

# Bibliography

There are various collections of Norse stories which give fuller accounts but with great variations. Unfortunately not all are in print at the present time.

Crossley-Holland, Kevin. *The Norse Myths*. New York: Pantheon Books, 1980.

•Green, Roger Lancelyn. *Myths of the Norsemen*. Harmondsworth, England: Penguin Books, 1970. First published in 1960 under the title: *The Saga of Asgard*.

Guerber, Hélene Adeline. *Myths of The Norsemen: from the eddas and the sagas.* New York: Dover Publications, 1992.

Keary, Annie. *The Heroes of Asgard: tales from Scandinavian Mythology*. Great Neck, New York: Core Collection Books, 1976.

Mackenzie, Donald Alexander. *Teutonic Myth and Legend.* New York: Avenel Books, 1985. Distributed by Crown Publishers.

Wilmot-Burton, Ethel Mary. *Told by the Northmen*. New York: T.Y. Crowell, 1908.

Wyatt, Isabel. *Thorkill of Iceland: Viking Hero-Tales*. Edinburgh: Floris Books, 1997.

• Recommended

Only one book of Rudolf Steiner's deals specifically with the Norse stories. This is *The Mission of Folk Souls*. It is difficult reading for anyone not versed in Steiner's world outlook. A fundamental book in this respect is Rudolf Steiner's *Occult Science: An Outline* (also published under the title *An Outline of Esoteric Science)*. The newcomer may find the author's booklets on Basic Anthroposophy a useful introduction.

## About the Author

Roy Wilkinson has been connected with the work of Rudolf Steiner for over 60 years. Born in Leicestershire, England, he was educated both locally and in Switzerland. He attended the Goetheanum School of Speech and Drama, receiving his certificate from Frau Dr. Steiner herself.

After working at an educational center, he made excursions into the fields of medicine (with Weleda) and agriculture, and eventually became a teacher. Over some forty years he taught in Steiner and State schools in England, Germany, and Switzerland. He has also taught children in need of special care.

Mr. Wilkinson has been active as an advisor to schools and lecturer on Rudolf Steiner education and Anthroposophy in many European countries, in South America as well as in English-speaking countries.

Another major contribution is the writing he has done over a period of more than twenty years. Wilkinson has produced introductory books on Rudolf Steiner education and its philosophical foundations. These and his curriculum guide booklets have been highly appreciated by teachers, parents, and those seeking answers to personal questions. A complete list of current editions is at the end of this volume.

## BOOKS BY ROY WILKINSON

**Questions and Answers on Rudolf Steiner Education**
**The Temperaments in Education**
**The Interpretation of Fairy Tales**
**The Curriculum of the Rudolf Steiner School**
**Commonsense Schooling**

**Wilkinson Waldorf Curriculum Series:**
Teaching English
Teaching Mathematics
Teaching Physics and Chemistry
Teaching Geography
Teaching History I: *Ancient Civilizations, Greece, Rome*
Teaching History II: *Middle Ages, Renaissance to Second World War*
Old Testament Stories
Commentary on the Old Testament Stories
The Norse Stories and Their Significance
Teaching Practical Activities: *Farming, Gardening, Housebuilding*
The Human Being and the Animal World
Plant Study and Geology
Nutrition, Health, and Anthropology
Miscellany: *A Collection of Poems and Plays*
Plays for Puppets

**The Origin and Development of Language**
**The Spiritual Basis of Rudolf Steiner Education**

**Rudolf Steiner: Aspects of his spiritual world view**
Anthroposophy vol. I: *Rudolf Steiner. Reincarnation and karma. The Spiritual Nature of the human being. The development of human consciousness.*
Anthroposophy vol. II: *Evolution of the world and humanity. Relationships between the living and the dead. Forces of evil. The modern path of initiation.*
Anthroposophy vol. III: *Life between death and rebirth. The spiritual hierarchies. The philosophical approach to the spirit. The mission of Christ.*

**May be Ordered from**: Rudolf Steiner College Bookstore
9200 Fair Oaks Boulevard
Fair Oaks, CA 95628, USA
Tel: (916) 961-8729 — Fax: (916) 961-3032